HOW TO
OVERCOME FEAR

HOW TO OVERCOME FEAR

And Live Your Life to the Fullest

MARCOS WITT

ATRIA BOOKS

New York   London   Toronto   Sydney

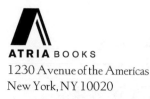

ATRIA BOOKS
1230 Avenue of the Americas
New York, NY 10020

Library of Congress Cataloging-in-Publication Data

Witt, Marcos.
   [Dile adiós a tus temores. English]
   How to overcome fear : and live life to the fullest / Marcos Witt ; [translated by
Amy Greenberg].
      p.   cm.
   1. Fear—Religious aspects—Christianity.   I. Title.
BV4908.5.W58513 2007
152.4'6—dc22   2006103161
ISBN-13: 978-0-7432-9084-5

First Atria Books hardcover edition March 2007

10 9 8 7 6 5 4 3 2 1

ATRIA BOOKS is a trademark of Simon & Schuster, Inc.

Manufactured in the United States of America

For information about special discounts for bulk purchases,
please contact Simon & Schuster Special Sales:
1-800-456-6798 or business@simonandschuster.com.

DEDICATION

I dedicate this book to the Hispanic congregation that meets every week in Lakewood Church to learn how to live like winners. You are a great inspiration to me. Your passion for being agents of positive change in our culture is one of the reasons why I pledge from week to week to improve my communications and offer you better messages.

This book began as a series of talks I gave to the congregation in the year 2003. Now I deliver this work to you so that with renewed and firm zeal you can leave behind your fear. My wife, Miriam, and I love you and are committed to your growth in the Lord. Our wish is that you may be filled with grace and wisdom.

CONTENTS

CONTENTS

CHAPTER TEN

The Only Valid Fear 179

FOREWORD

by Joel Osteen

Fear can be one of the most debilitating aspects of life; it incapacitates some people, and robs love, joy, and effectiveness from millions of others. Fear can plunder your self-esteem; it can keep you from living at your full potential and trap you in a self-constructed prison.

Fear often breeds in ignorance—ignorance of the facts, ignorance of God's love, and ignorance of God's Word. We tend to be afraid of that with which we are unfamiliar. It's easy to be intimidated by the unknown, of people, places, or experiences that are different from our own. If you allow it, fear will devastate your present and destroy your future.

That's why I am delighted that my dear friend and colleague Marcos Witt has written this liberating book. In *How to Overcome Fear*, you will discover how to confront fear directly; you will find keys to help you determine what your fear is and why you are afraid. Most important of all, Marcos will help you to focus your attention on God and His love, power, and promises to help you. Marcos shows you how to deal with phobias, anxiety, and panic and that ominous sense that "all is not well." He points you to specific answers in God's Word that pertain to your fear, and shows you how to use those Scriptures to defeat fear through praise.

I've known Marcos Witt personally for a number of years, and it has been my pleasure to work closely with him and to consider him a true friend. He is a man of faith and integrity with a God-given gift to communicate. I have seen the principles contained in his book work firsthand. And I know that if you will do your part, God will use Marcos Witt's insights to help you triumph over your fears, and live the life of victory that God has in store for you.

HOW TO OVERCOME FEAR

Understand and Conquer

Nothing in life is to be feared.
It is only to be understood.

—MARIE CURIE

Snakes and Ladders

The sensation I felt was much more than simple fear or fright: It was pure *terror*! It was a night like any other, nearing time to go to sleep in the bedroom I shared with my two brothers. After dinner and helping with a few household chores, I was getting ready to climb the stairs to our bedroom. It was not a big house. I lived there with my parents, my two brothers, and my twin sisters. Just three bedrooms and one and a half baths. My sisters shared the room next to my parents' on the first floor. On the second floor, there was a big room that we used for playing, reading, and studying. Normally, this was what you would call "the TV room," but there was no television. Crossing over, you arrived at the door to our bedroom, with its half bath and the bunk beds where my brothers and I slept. To reach the second floor, you had to open a door to one side of the kitchen and climb a flight of stairs. These stairs were no more than slabs of concrete held up by iron brackets. Between each step, you could see the darkness beneath the stairs, a space where my mother stored things. We rarely accessed this space and didn't have much desire to enter it.

One night, I confidently opened the door that led to the second floor, noting that the hallway light was off. I thought nothing of it because I knew there was a light switch next to the stairs that I could turn on. What happened next was something that has remained etched in my memory. When I put my foot down on the first step, I felt movement under the stairs. My eyes were drawn to the darkness beneath them. Once I realized something out of the ordinary was happening, my heart started beating fast. Suddenly, I saw a hand reach out from between the steps and grab my ankle. I let out a terrifying scream that could be heard all the way down the block. My two brothers had hidden themselves among the boxes underneath the stairs and waited patiently to play their scary prank.

Thirty-two years have passed since that day (I am forty-three years old as I write this) and I can still feel the anguish of that horrible moment. I collapsed on the floor, my body shaking like a leaf in the wind, my breathing rapid and short, my heart beating a mile a minute. The only sound louder than the beating of my heart was the laughter of my brothers, who found their act very funny. I can assure you that very few times in my life have I felt such absolute panic. After that incident, I mounted those stairs with true anxiety, and I always made sure, before going up, that there was no one hiding beneath them.

We all have our own stories, right? Vivid moments, dark memories, moments of panic and total distress. Life gives us thousands of opportunities to face our fears. There's no way around it. It's part of our daily existence. However, what we do with these opportunities determines whether we will overcome our fear or keep on living within its chains. Many people live completely controlled by their fears, doubts, phobias, anxieties, bad omens, and bouts of nerves. But it doesn't have to be that way. There is good news: We can live in freedom! We can live calmly, safely, and without fear of anyone or anything.

As a child, I remember playing a board game named Snakes and Ladders. The board depicted figures of snakes and ladders superimposed on blocks that contained numbers. The object was to reach the goal by tossing a little die that told us the number of spaces we could advance, or sometimes, depending on where the game piece fell, go back. The neck of a snake could land us on a position much farther along on the board or just as easily return us to the start. A ladder could help us win a higher or lower number, depending on the numbers the die showed and where our game piece landed. I recalled this game when I thought of my experience on the staircase and of my other great fear: snakes.

It's very likely I inherited it from my mom. She was always very afraid of snakes. But when I speak of fear, I am not talking about just any fear, but of something way beyond the norm. My mother could probably handle any event in life except confronting a snake. Just like me! I was so afraid of snakes, that I couldn't even watch them in a movie or look at them in photos, and it didn't matter if they were dead or behind glass. I couldn't stand them any way at all. If I happened to see a snake, emotions ran throughout my entire body: a mixture of desperation, anxiety, fright, revulsion, and pure fear. My reaction was not only one of psychological fear, but a very real physical reaction. I felt something like a shiver running through my whole being. My heart beat faster, my breath was short, and my pupils dilated.

In the same house where I had the experience with the stairs, we had a large backyard. My brothers and I used to spend hours playing in the yard with our dog and our toys. Since the house was in the country, we were surrounded by several acres of uninhabited land. Consequently, we often saw many different repulsive wild animals, especially country rodents, rats and the like. You could see snakes once in a while, too. I will never forget when we helped my mother clear the garden and my sister Jeannie and I were working on one side of the house, pulling out tall, dry grass. Underneath this grass was a small garter snake that bit my three-year-old sister's hand. My sister was annoyed by the prick and ran to tell us that a "mama worm" had bitten her. She didn't know that what bit her was a snake. I reached the scene of the crime to see a green snake slither to its hiding place. It left a terrorized group of humans in its wake, and I almost saw it smile derisively at all of us. My father wasn't home, so I took my sister by bicycle to the doctor's office, a few blocks from our house. Mom caught up to us on foot. Thank God, it was nothing serious and my sister was soon back home.

In this same backyard, my father had asked me to move a stack of bricks that some workers had left there to a less visible spot. I spent more than fifteen minutes moving bricks and was happy to finally be nearing the last ones because, truth be told, I didn't much want to be moving them in the first place. What I wanted to do was to play with my friends. When I reached for the last brick, I suddenly noticed the two disgusting black eyes watching me carefully from the lawn. It was a big fat snake, brown with black stripes and ugly deep-set eyes that looked at me with distrust, almost as if scolding me for interrupting his afternoon nap. It didn't take me even a millisecond to react. I threw the bricks on the ground and began running as fast as I could yelling forcefully: "Dad, Dad . . . a snake . . . big . . . ugly . . . angry . . ." Within seconds everyone came out of the house, my father with an ax, searching for a way to flush out the snake and kill it.

To be truthful, I don't remember the end of the story, if they killed it or not; I couldn't stay nearby because of the fear I felt. For as long as we lived in that house, I could not approach that spot again.

The snakes and ladders in my life have marked me forever. And I can assure you that it isn't some game. The only thing that gives me the authority to speak on the subject of fear is that I have fought against it all my life. In one way or another, I have always had to contend with it and come out ahead in spite of the many times it has wanted to immobilize me. Fear is something so real, it has debilitated millions of people, preventing them from reaching their life goals, objectives, and ideals. But not you. You will overcome your fears. You will escape from this jail and turn into a great champion of life.

KNOW AND CONQUER

The great historian Tito Livio said the following: "We fear things in proportion to our ignorance of them." Most people have great fears due to a lack of knowledge. For example, most animals are more afraid of us than we are of them. It took me many years to realize that the snake I came upon under the brick that sunny afternoon in Durango, Mexico, must have been much more afraid of me than I was of it. After all, I was one hundred times its size, and had discovered its hiding place, leaving it vulnerable to attack. When you and I are afraid of something or someone, they seem bigger and more frightening than they really are. That snake, because of how much I feared it, seemed larger and more threatening than she actually was. What was I lacking? More knowledge of snakes. It's that simple. The Great Teacher of all time, Jesus, expressed it even better: "Then you will know the truth and the truth shall set you free" (John 8:32). The more we know the truth, the freer we will be of fear.

My life changed as the result of making a decision. I confess that it wasn't an easy decision, but a worthwhile one. I was enjoying an afternoon with my children, watching a television program called *The Crocodile Hunter*, starring the late, daring Australian animal expert Steve Irwin. My three sons, like my daughter, Elena, had always been fascinated by nature, especially wildlife. From a very young age, they read books and studied encyclopedias about animals. Steve Irwin's program was one of their favorites. Suddenly, this man's adventures with crocodiles and dangerous lizards no longer satisfied him, so he began to expand his horizons to include reptiles of every kind, including dangerous snakes and serpents. Without my knowing this last bit of information, I was watching the program, when suddenly, an enormous, brightly colored serpent appeared on the screen. It was a long creature, oily-looking and silent, and Irwin was holding it by its tail, lifting it toward the sky, while the snake's head was down near the floor, trying with all its might to escape. Immediately, I began to feel the same sensation I felt my whole life when confronted with the image or presence of a snake: goose bumps, rapid heartbeat, shortness of breath, tingling along my whole spine, etc. My children, who had known of my fear of snakes their whole lives, began teasing me: "Look, Dad—what a pretty snake! Do you like it? Look how it moves. Would you like it wrapped around your neck?" and so on. They burst out laughing at my terrified reaction. It was something I couldn't help. Something I had lived with my entire life. I was thirty-five years old at that point, and here my kids were, making fun of me!

At that moment, I made a decision and I didn't hesitate a second in deciding it. I forced myself to watch that TV show, despite all the symptoms I felt throughout my body. I couldn't stand having that fear one minute longer and the time had come to do something about it. I decided the only way to get rid of this phobia was to get closer to that which I feared, to understand it better. And that is what I did.

Today I can say that I am totally free from my fear of snakes. I've proven it on the many occasions that we've gone to the zoo as a family, when I do something I'd never done before: enter the reptile building and stay inside to learn about the snakes: where they came from, what they liked to eat, and other interesting facts. When I learned more about the reptile world, I discovered that the vast majority of vipers attack only when threatened. If we leave them alone, they'll leave us alone. I have decided that I can live tranquilly doing this.

The truth is what set me free with regard to snakes. The truth is what will set you free from the fear that oppresses you. The closer we get to understand our fears, the more we realize the lie hidden behind them. Tito Livio said, "Fear always wants to see things as worse than they are." How true are his words.

A Success Story: My friend Betty Santiesteban lives in the
city of Durango, where I grew up. Our city is world famous
for its scorpions. Not because they are big, ugly, or hideously
colored, but because they carry a fatal venom. Scorpions can
be found all over the world, but few are as dangerous as those
in our dear Durango. Certain parts of the city are home to
more scorpions than other parts. One of these areas is the
neighborhood of Remedios Hill, where, back then, my friends
Betty and Chava Santiesteban lived. Betty recalls that in the
mornings, before putting on her shoes, she always checked
them to make sure that a scorpion hadn't hidden inside them.
Occasionally, she opened a drawer and there would be a
scorpion in full defense mode: tail up, pincers ready to
grab, poised to inject its fatal poison into any aggressor
who disturbed it. Every day Betty encountered scorpions—
sometimes dozens a day. The problem was, she suffered
from a serious scorpion phobia. They terrorized her, and
that did not make for a very peaceful life.

One day, Betty read the words of Our Lord Jesus:
"Know the truth and the truth shall set you free." She
decided to learn everything there was to know about
scorpions. Upon inquiring, she found that little had
been written on the subject, so she began interviewing
professionals who treat scorpion victims. She searched
the state library and read magazines and periodicals to find
any articles she could on the subject. From this research she
compiled a great many facts, and began to put them together
in a book. Her original plan was to get to know the world of

scorpions to help herself, but the result was something even greater: the publication of her notes and drawings in two books have helped thousands of people overcome their fear of scorpions. By trying to "know the truth," Betty became an expert on the subject. Such has been her acclaim that when the National Geographic Channel wanted to make a documentary about dangerous scorpions, they called Betty Santiesteban, a simple housewife who decided to overcome her fear by knowing the truth. Hers is a true success story, just like yours will become.

FACE IT

There is no way to avoid it: We will all be faced with situations that frighten us. The only way to come out ahead is to know the truth that will set us free. It is vital that each one of us makes the decision to say "Enough! I'm tired of feeling afraid. Today I will change my way of thinking and do something about it." The fact is, you may *feel* fear, but you needn't lie down and give in to it. If we flee, we will never be victorious against anything. In fact, if we look at how soldiers are armed, we see that their principal armor is on the front of their bodies. Why? Because that is the part of them that will be exposed. Conquering warriors always face their enemies. A coward always runs away. You and I have but one option: Face fear once and for all.

I am an avid student of the Bible. I encounter many positive examples among the figures on its pages, along with practical advice that serves me well in my daily life. One of the most well known biblical characters is young David. He became one of the greatest warriors and most respected kings of all time. Even as a young boy his dynamism and charisma set him apart. Since childhood, he confronted challenges that most boys his age never met. Charged with tending his father Jesse's sheep, he often had to free them from the claws of wild animals that tried to invade and eat the small herd. One time he killed a bear and a lion that wanted to kill his sheep. It was a show of force, determination, and singular bravery for a young man of around fifteen. Surely, he must have had moments of panic and despair, but instead of turning his back on these challenges, he faced them. He did not flee. Surely David could never have imagined that these fights with wild animals would be part of his preparation for the biggest test of his life.

His enemy Goliath was a formidable fellow. Measuring nearly ten feet tall, he was the paladin of the Philistines' army. What's more, he was rude, foulmouthed, and defiant. So much so that the entire Israelite army hid in their encampments every time this brash man came out to challenge them, demanding that someone come forth to fight him. Even King Saul, the supposed commander-in-chief of the troops, was unable to deal with this grave situation. Without a plan, and without bravery in their hearts, the army was paralyzed before the mocking Goliath. He appeared daily to laugh in their faces, provoking more panic and terror in the hearts of his opponents. A cowardly king, paralyzed soldiers, a formidable enemy, and a lack of direction made this situation a great impasse in every respect.

One day the young shepherd David arrived. It would not take him long to realize something was terribly wrong in the soldiers' camp. There he found a pair of his brothers, who were the reason for his visit. His father had directed him to bring a meal to them. When his brothers saw him, they were angry at him, for they deemed the situation far too dangerous for a "child" his age. Strange, because there could not be danger in a place where nothing was happening, and in this supposed "field of battle," nothing was happening. Nonetheless, they angrily tried to convince David to go back home.

Just then Goliath appeared on the scene, as he did at that time every day, to begin his daily ritual of mockery and provocation. When David saw him and heard what was going on, he grew indignant at this powerful, filthy man who dared to mock the army of the people of God. His anger was such that he offered to be the warrior who would take him on. Suddenly he found himself before King Saul, explaining why he would make a good candidate to go before this mocker who insulted them to no end. Seeing no alternative, Saul sent him to meet the enemy with little more than a blessing and the hope that Goliath wouldn't annihilate him.

This is the part of the story that grabs my attention because it's the part that will most help you and me overcome our fears. Certainly David understood the gravity of the situation. Surely, he took measure of Goliath's size. He knew that everything rested on his shoulders, that the fate of thousands of soldiers depended on the success or failure of his plan. All his life, David demonstrated prudence and appropriateness in all that he did, and despite his being so young, we can't imagine that he lacked that same good sense on this occasion, too. My feeling is that David walked toward that giant with his knees shaking, with his heart racing a mile a minute, with sweat on his brow, yet confident, because he knew that inside of him was a great force—the force of the Lord—that would help him destroy this enormous adversary. David went forth to meet Goliath *in spite of* what his fears and emotions were telling him. At all times, he knew that a force greater than himself was going to help him out of this jam.

When the giant made fun of David and even got angry at him, having expected a more formidable opponent, David answered his insults with declarations of victory—not in his own name nor in the name of the people of Israel, but in God's name, in the name of God Almighty, captain of the heavenly hosts. The boy David understood that the only one who can free us from our enemies, our fears, and our afflictions is the Lord, Our Father. He is more than ready to help us out of any situation. Nevertheless, David also understood that he had to do *his* part. This is what many of us forget. We want God to say some magic words, move His wand toward the sky, and—*poof!*—everything is fixed. Most of the time, it doesn't work that way. We have to do our part, and the Lord does what we are not able to do. It is a collaboration between the two. David understood this. He had already entrusted himself to God and he was ready for whatever came next. As soon as he readied his weapon (his small sling-shot), his munitions (five little round stones lifted from a nearby streambed), he armed himself with bravery and went forth to meet his enemy.

"David hurried and ran to the battle line" (1 Samuel 17:48). I want to focus on this sentence because it says a lot about why David faced and conquered his fears, something from which we can all learn a lesson. In this sentence we see David's attitude in the face of challenge. It is a proactive attitude, of intervening in the matter right now and not letting another second go by without solving the problem: "He ran." David had determined that this problem had gone on for too long and he wasn't going to let things remain as they were for one second more. So he began to run to the battlefront instead of going on with his life, denying the existence of the problem, and hiding within the safety of an encampment, like the rest of his compatriots did.

Most of us who have battled all our lives with some kind of fear have not faced it with the speed necessary to cut down the problem in its earliest stage. Many times, because of our indecision, the problem grows out of proportion, bringing us to a crisis that destroys our emotions, our families, our friends, and our worlds. We have to be like David: Once we recognize a problem, we must run to the front lines, face the great giant in our lives, and immediately right the situation so we can go on living in peace. Like David, we will find that our action, and our trust in the Lord, will have great results in our personal, professional, and emotional lives. We will see our own huge Goliaths fall, just as David saw his. And we will taste the sweet food of triumph.

Hurry! Run to the front lines of battle! The fact that you hold this book in your hands shows me that you are a person who will overcome your fears and know how to deal wisely with every giant that shows up in your life.

It's a Matter of Deciding

The reason the Israelites were freed from Goliath was that among them was a person so fed up that he did something about it. What will make you and me victorious is a permanent, immovable decision to battle every giant we encounter. Some of these giants will greatly intimidate us. Some of them will truly make us feel incapable of functioning. Others will make fun of us and say all manner of insults to us. But we have to decide, this very day, to run quickly to the battlefront and face each one with determination and character, knowing that the Force of the All-Powerful resides within each of us and will help us win. If we trust in Him, we will drink of His strengths and be able to triumphantly face any challenge. It's all a matter of deciding.

Some of us have grown so accustomed to fear that it has become part of our daily lives. Our vocabulary incorporates fear. For example, I often hear people say, "I'm afraid my children won't turn out well," or "I'm afraid my husband is cheating on me," or "I'm worried I'll never get ahead at work," or "I fear I'll never pay off this debt," or "I'm worried I'll never overcome this bad habit that I've had for so long," or "I'm afraid our family will never rise out of poverty." I'm afraid, I'm afraid, I'm afraid . . . To overcome our fears, we will have to change our vocabulary. Our words are powerful: They can build or destroy. Every time we say "I'm afraid that . . ." we are driving the stake of fear deeper into our hearts. Every time we articulate the fear in our lives, we are affirming it and making room for it, instead of destroying it and getting it out of our hearts forever.

We all know the story of Job. From one day to the next, he lost everything: his house, his family, his possessions, his money, property, riches—everything. It is interesting to note that during the first few days that he faced this big test, we hear him say the following: "What I feared has come upon me; what I dreaded has happened to me" (Job 3:25). Fear was in his daily vocabulary, so when it arrived, he wasn't surprised because he'd been fearing it his whole life. What a great example of why we should watch what we say! By changing the way we speak we begin the journey of overcoming our fears. Make an honest appraisal. Is fear in your vocabulary? Do you use declarations of fear in your daily conversation? Do you use words of anxiety and oppression? Change your vocabulary *today.*

Changing our vocabulary will change our mind-set. We have to change our way of thinking. If we keep thinking that our fears will destroy and overcome us, that is what will happen. If we think we'll be just fine and that there are better days ahead, that is what will happen. The old proverb says: "However a man thinks in his heart, thus he is" (Proverbs 23:7). If we think we can overcome our fears, we will do so. If we think tomorrow will be a better day, it will be. If we can think we are victorious warriors, we will be. First, we have to conquer our own minds before we can overcome anything else. Many times, we are our own worst enemies.

In 1963, Jim Whittaker became the first North American to reach the summit of Mount Everest. Few have had the good fortune to make it there. Whittaker wrote, "One never conquers a mountain. Mountains cannot be conquered. One conquers oneself, one's expectations and fears." The result of overcoming oneself is that we can scale the highest peaks life gives us. We can enjoy life's pleasures. God designed it this way. He gave us all of creation to enjoy. Unfortunately, many of us haven't overcome our own doubts and fears to enjoy the abundance that God has given each of us. Decide today that you won't be one of those people. "Better a patient man than a warrior, one who controls his temper than one who takes a city" (Proverbs 16:32). Decide today that you will conquer your thoughts and become a great warrior, enjoying the life that God Our Father has given us in His kindness and compassion.

Changing our habits and our vocabulary will help us change our perceptions. For example, I can now watch television shows about snakes without feeling anything at all. What a switch from a few years ago. I decided, I got close to my fear (I ran to the front line of battle), I changed my vocabulary (I stopped saying that snakes frighten me), I changed my mentality (I started telling myself I could overcome this fear), and I changed my habits (I can now see photos, television programs, and live snakes with no reaction). Having said all this, I assure you I haven't reached the level of wanting to live with them. I respect them, and I am not afraid of them, but

I'm happy they have their place and that in most cases, our worlds don't collide.

In conclusion, if you get closer to your fears and come to understand them, you'll be able to overcome them. To do this you must understand the truth about who you are and about the marvelous power that the Lord has put in your life. Keep trying to know the truth; it will set you free. The pastor and writer Robert Schuller once said, "If you listen to your fears, you will die without ever knowing how great you could have been." You are a great person, and I am sure you are beginning one of the best journeys of your life.

Reflection

1. Do I have a fearful vocabulary?

2. What can I do to change my way of speaking?

3. What can I do to get closer to my fears and know them better, so that I can overcome them?

4. Which habits, attitudes, and thoughts of mine could I change to overcome my fears?

5. What can I do to "race to the battlefront" to conquer my fears?

Prayer

God and Heavenly Father: Help me leave my fears behind. I beg You not to let me fear the journey itself. I beg You to give me the strength and determination to change my way of speaking, thinking, and acting as it relates to fear. I want to have the necessary resolve to race to the battlefront to conquer the fears in my life. I trust in You and in Your power to carry me forward. Thank You for Your strength.

CHAPTER TWO

Phobias, Fears, and Panic Attacks

The only thing we have to fear is fear itself.

—FRANKLIN DELANO ROOSEVELT

It happened in the international airport of Bogotá, Colombia. We had taken part in a three-day multitudinous event in their enclosed stadium, El Campín. I had sung, given various lectures, done many interviews and other activities. I was exhausted. Adding to that, in those years (1994 to 1996), I was going through a fairly difficult time in my personal life. I was dealing with a type of constant depression that I neither understood nor knew how to fight. I would end a concert or lecture and return to my hotel sad, discouraged, crying, and confused. In spite of the fact that all the activities had been spectacular, and many people had been touched by the message and music of God, I was fighting one of the greatest battles of my life. Later, I realized that it was the convergence of several factors that brought me to this state of total discouragement. The main factor was that my schedule involved so much work, in so many cities, without rest or even time to breathe, that my body was rebelling fiercely against this fast pace. Thank God that with the help of a great Christian psychologist, Dr. Doug Weiss, I was able to understand that my problem wasn't psychological, but rather physical. The day that Dr. Weiss opened my eyes to my condition was a great day in my life. However, many years would pass before I understood what had happened to me in the Bogotá airport.

When we were just a few minutes from boarding the plane, I had what I now know was a panic attack. My breathing sped up, my hands began to sweat, I felt as if I couldn't breathe, and my heart beat rapidly. From the spot where I was seated, away from the other passengers, I could see the airplane on the other side of the glass wall, and it made me feel panicky. I felt sure the plane would crash, that we would never arrive home, and would all wind up dead. The more I thought about it, the surer I was that this would happen. My desperation increased when I saw some of my band members begin boarding. My eyes filled with tears. My frustration grew with the impotence that flooded through me.

Two of my companions, Alfonso Ortiz and Melvin Cruz, saw me from afar and suddenly realized something was wrong. By the time they reached me, I was a total disaster. I felt an unbearable sensation of suffocating. An enormous pressure in my chest made me feel as if I would die. When I explained what was happening, they very patiently each took one of my hands and began to pray. They thanked God for His angels who protect us. They thanked Him for the privilege of having been at this beautiful event in Bogotá, where so many lives had been touched and transformed by the Lord's powerful love. They thanked God for me, and they began to pray against this overwhelming fear. Their voices and the content of their prayers were the two things that brought me back to reality. It was practically miraculous. I immediately began to feel a strong sense of peace. I looked again at the plane outside, and the very same scene that had just provoked such a fearful, negative sensation now filled me with the joy of knowing that this vehicle would take me home to my precious wife, Miriam, and my children. My breathing began returning to normal. My heart started beating normally again. That dark moment had passed. I got up, dried my tears, and proceeded to the gate, knowing that, come what may, God held my life in His powerful hands.

That flight arrived at its destination without a single problem, and I thought of when Winston Churchill recounted the story of the old man who had a lot of trouble in his life, most of which never happened.

Why Are We Afraid?

Fear is a sensation produced in reaction to an object, person, or event. It is the result of a logical worry, directly related to something or someone. For example, when we see a train coming as our car is crossing the tracks, we feel a rational fear, directly related to that object (the train) and a real act (its coming toward us). A related sensation is the worry that appears like an alarm, warning us of the imminent approach of danger. It has the same effect as a yellow light saying, "Let's pause. Let's immediately take all possible precautions." For example, when we near the edge of a great precipice, our body produces an alarm, saying: "Don't take another step. There's danger ahead." On the other hand, phobia is an intense focus on a specific object or situation that produces an extreme anxiety that we feel much more strongly than fear.

Our brain produces chemicals called neurotransmitters that serve to maintain the balance between a normal state and a sense of danger. When the brain detects that our body is in danger, it warns us in milliseconds so we can adequately prepare to face it. For example, if we stop suddenly on the edge of a rooftop, our brain realizes we are in danger and, in that instant, it tells our body that if we don't maintain a certain distance, we run the risk of falling. This causes our legs to take a few steps backward. In this case, the neurotransmitters help us make a positive, important decision instantly. The problem comes when those important chemicals produce a feeling of panic when there is no imminent danger. Many people who suffer fears and phobias in their daily lives have this chemical imbalance.

A *simple phobia* is the fear of specific objects or situations. In the case of my friend Betty Santiesteban, scorpions. Among these phobias are claustrophobia (fear of enclosed spaces) and acrophobia (fear of heights). Many of these simple phobias are the result of experiences we had when we were young. I, until this day, have a slight fear of enclosed spaces. If I am in an elevator full of people, I feel short of breath and a bit desperate. Another thing I discovered is my aversion to flying while seated between two strangers. The times I've been in this situation, I feel a slight desperation. I have never analyzed why I have this condition, but it probably has to do with something that happened to me as a small child.

Another well-known phobia is agoraphobia. This is the fear of being helpless in public places, like shopping centers, the theater, the subway, or other places from which it is difficult to escape. Many who suffer from this phobia become hermits, opting to stay shut up in their homes rather than go out where there may be a lot of people. The experts say this kind of phobia begins to develop during youth and adolescence.

More common than agoraphobia are social phobias. These are the fears of looking foolish or feeling ashamed in public. We have all had one of those dreams where we find ourselves naked in public, suffering great shame on the streets as we try desperately to hurry home to get dressed. Many times I have dreamed that I am appearing onstage dressed only in my underwear. The thought panics me. Every time I have the dream, in the dream itself I wonder, Why do I have to dream this? Why is this happening to me? while everyone in the audience laughs at me. Thank God, this has happened to me only in dreams. One of my close relatives has a mild phobia like this. He doesn't like attending weddings or meetings with a lot of people, or spending a lot of time in crowds. He'd much prefer to be at home with his family, surrounded by people who love him and among whom he feels safe. He also has a hard time meeting new people.

Panic attacks, on the other hand, are the result of an "alarm system" that the Lord gave our bodies to let us know when danger is coming and how we should correctly confront it. However, when the alarm system doesn't work properly, it causes panic attacks. We may feel rapid or violent palpitations, dizziness, nausea, chest pains, trouble breathing, suffocation, chills, dreamlike sensations, and fear of death, among other things. Many people who suffer frequent panic attacks are more inclined to seek refuge in alcohol, drugs, or other types of addictions to quell their fear. People who suffer panic attacks tend toward a greater incidence of suicide. They need help. It is a real condition, with real symptoms and consequences. What must be done is to correct this out-of-control internal alarm system. What happened to me in the Bogotá airport was a panic attack. Once my alarm system was fixed, I was able to return to normal. I've needed to fix my alarm system several times. But here's the good news: It can be fixed! One doesn't have to live with fear, phobias, terror, or panic attacks.

There are so many phobias that it would be impossible to write a list long enough to include them all. My intention in listing them is simply to illustrate their range and number. If you suffer from any of these conditions, you can rest assured there is a solution to your problem.

We won't run out of phobias. There are hundreds, perhaps thousands of them. I have included some that are curious or else slightly funny.

He who fears that he will suffer, already suffers from his fear.

—M. DE MONTAIGNE

Nephophobia: fear of clouds

Nudophobia: fear of nudity

Ombrophobia: fear of rain

Ommetaphobia: fear of eyes

Patroiophobia: fear of inheritance

Anthrophobia: fear of flowers

Ailurophobia: fear of cats

Acarophobia: fear of itching

Clinophobia: fear of going to bed

Doraphobia: fear of skins of animals or furs

Photophobia: fear of light

Peniaphobia : fear of poverty

Rhabdophobia : fear of magic

Satanophobia : fear of Satan

Tachophobia : fear of speed (not fear of tacos)

Arithmophobia : fear of numbers

Theophobia : fear of gods

Melophobia : fear of music (I have never had this)

Telephonophobia : fear of telephones (very rarely found among
women)

Vestiphobia : fear of clothing

Zoophobia : fear of animals

Panophobia : fear of everything

FAMOUS PEOPLE AND THEIR FEARS

Phobias don't discriminate. History tells of many well-known individuals who have fought all their lives against fears and phobias.
Caesar Augustus, for example, the great Roman emperor, was afraid
of the dark. Henry III, king of France, was afraid of cats. Queen Eliz-
abeth I of England was deathly afraid of roses. The renowned psychiatrist Sigmund Freud was scared to travel by train. He suffered panic
attacks at the very same time he was writing his famous works about

the neurosis anxiety. Natalie Wood, the North American actress who won hearts around the world, had a great fear of water. Unfortunately, her tragic death by drowning involved that which she feared most. The great bullfighter César Rincón was scared of rats. It's incredible that this man could be in a ring with a bull weighing more than a ton, yet couldn't bear to be in the presence of a rodent that weighed less than his boots. This is how phobias work: without discrimination, and usually without rhyme or reason. All we know is that one way or another, we all suffer from some type of fear that we need to overcome.

The winner of the 2004 Nobel Prize for Literature, Elfriede Jelinek, could not attend the award ceremony because of her profound social phobia. To explain why she couldn't attend this meeting, she said only that "It would cause me more desperation than happiness." After becoming very well known, she moved from her home because too many people found out her address and that terrorized her.

In 1967 the singer Barbra Streisand, before a huge audience in New York's Central Park, forgot the words to a song. That caused her such panic and frustration that she stopped performing in public for many years. It wasn't until 1994, twenty-seven years later, that Streisand gave another public concert.

Johnny Depp, the actor who has starred in some of the greatest hit movies of the last few years (*Pirates of the Caribbean, Charlie and the Chocolate Factory*), admits to having a fear of heights. Incredibly, in some of his scenes in *Pirates*, he had to be suspended from great heights on the ship for long periods of time. However, Depp did not let his phobia win out over him. Rather, he took it in hand and defeated it.

Oprah Winfrey is one of the best-known women in the world, as a businesswoman, an interviewer, a philanthropist, an actress, and an author. She grew up in total poverty, in a broken home, lost in confusion. Oprah has spoken openly about the abuse she suffered, her difficult childhood, and how when she later went to live with her father, she found in him all that she had been lacking: discipline, maturity, and stability. At the beginning of her career she had to overcome not only the fears associated with being one of the first African-American women to break into the field she chose, but of being ridiculed for being overweight. She speaks of the uneasiness she felt making decisions, but these decisions were critical to the success of her career. In her own words, Oprah says, "The thing you fear most has no power over you. Your *fear* of it is what has power over you."

The list of persons throughout history, both ancient and modern, who have had to overcome their fears and phobias is very long. Abraham Lincoln lived in a state of near-constant depression because of his great struggle against fear. The groundbreaking scientist Isaac Newton was so afraid of his colleagues' criticism that he delayed publishing his great discoveries.

Many people successfully overcome their fears; others do not. On one occasion, my wife, Miriam, and I found ourselves in New York City, participating in the last crusade of the renowned evangelist Billy Graham. The day we were to return home, we were driven to the airport by a young man who had always lived in that big city. Talking with him, we discovered a very interesting person who could comment about many different subjects related to life in the Big Apple. Suddenly, Miriam asked him about the events related to September 11, 2001. The question was innocent and in the spirit of good conversation. Within seconds, our driver underwent an 180-degree transformation. In a firm but low voice he told us without hesitation that this subject was off-limits. He went on to explain that for him, it was very difficult when people like ourselves, who hadn't lived in the city, dared to bring up such a sensitive subject so indiscreetly. Miriam and I immediately understood his message and looked for another subject of discussion, after offering him our sincere apologies. After much thought on the subject, I have reached the conclusion that that young driver had suffered such pain from the terrorist attacks that he still wasn't all right inside. Like many, he chose simply not to talk about it.

The brilliant playwright Tennessee Williams lived with paralyzing shyness, insomnia, and claustrophobia. Instead of facing his fears and seeking help, he tried to treat them with alcohol and pills. This merely brought him greater desperation and his life ended tragically.

But this will not happen to you, dear reader! The end of your story will be one of triumph and victory. With God's help, you will face each one of your fears and come out ahead. Once and for all, you will overcome your fears.

What to Do?

The first step is to recognize that a problem exists. The second step is to seek help. Most of us cannot face it alone. We need the help of someone who can see our situation objectively and ask the right questions to lead us to the answers that will bring us victory. One of the best decisions I made many years ago was to find myself a good counselor who could help me in a few areas of my life where I was confused. The ability to answer his questions, listen to his advice, and receive his prayers has been elemental in my ability to confront and overcome these perplexities. The question you have to ask yourself is: Are you sufficiently tired of living with fear? If you continue to coexist with a phobia, it will never leave your life, for it knows it is always welcome there. Be careful, because when you least expect it, fear will betray you and get the upper hand. Don't let things turn out this way. Ask God for the power to seek the help that will bring you a new lifestyle.

If you find yourself living with fear continually, seek professional help. If it's not very serious, seek the help of your pastor, spiritual leader, or a counselor familiar with the subject who could recommend material for you to read and give you good advice and mental exercises to help you reconstruct your life.

In his manuscript "It's All in Your Mind," Dr. Daniel Kennedy compares our past experiences ("outlines") that positively or negatively affect our present reactions, with movie scripts. Dr. Kennedy writes, "You are an actor, your life is a movie, and your outline is the script. Every time a situation comes up, you automatically react in accordance with your outline. The good news is that you are the author of your own screenplay. You can rewrite your outline and overcome your fears. In truth, it's not a process you can do on your own. But with the help of a therapist, an expert in theories such as relational emotive therapy or narrative therapy, you can erase the fears from your mind."

DIVINE HELP

The fields of medicine and science are pathways that lead many people to overcome their fears. However, one of the safest and most successful ways to erase your uncertainties and overcome your fears is found in the phrase "Tell it to the Lord." There is an incalculable force available to every one of us when we understand and embrace the fact that God is the one who sustains the Universe and that our lives are in His powerful hands. An unexplainable freedom derives from knowing that our future is being written by His hand, on His flight plan, in His ways. When we make peace with Him, everything else will have new meaning. We can view life from a new perspective, through a divine filter. This changes everything. When we understand that our past negative experiences have been left in His hands, we can live free of the past. When we understand that the betrayals and abandonment we have suffered have remained in His hands, we are no longer governed by fear, anxiety, impotence, revenge, or any of the adverse emotions that paralyze us. When we know that our errors have been left in His hands, we no longer need to fear, because we know that He has forgiven every one of our mistakes and has given us His hand so that we can walk with freedom and certainty in this life. The benefits are infinite when we find our life's compass in God our Father by way of a personal relationship with His Son Jesus Christ.

Jesus told His disciples, "Do not fear." He said these words to them because they, like us, had lived through times that would frighten anyone. One of these times was the night that Jesus Himself walked on water.

> *But to the fourth (quarter) vigil of the night, Jesus went to them walking on the lake. The disciples, seeing him walk on the lake were troubled, saying: A ghost!*
>
> *And they screamed with fright. But quickly Jesus spoke to them, saying: Have courage! It is me; do not fear.*
>
> MATTHEW 14:25—27

The disciples, who were rowing the boat, thought it was a vision. Upon hearing the voice of Jesus, they realized it was their teacher and became calm. Put yourself in their place. Any one of us would have felt frightened if we saw a man walking on water. It's natural. But Jesus is not natural, and for this reason His voice continues until this very day, declaring to all those who dare to believe Him and follow Him, "Do not fear . . . I am with you."

Dr. Francisco Contreras sent me a marvelous piece of writing with which I would like to close this chapter. Who better than God is there to help us overcome our phobias, fears, and panic? He created us, and He knows better than anyone how we function. He knows us much better than we know ourselves.

Do Not Be Afraid

BY DR. FRANCISCO CONTRERAS

Can we control fear? Fear is not only a mental state, but something very real and very physical. The genesis of panic lies in a chemical event that affects the neurological circuitry of the brain. Back in the 1920s, Walter Cannon, a Harvard psychologist, reported that small hormonal discharges cause the nervous system to react to danger in a physiological manner, and in this way, the body prepares for "fight or flight," which we recognize as a reaction to severe stress. We now know that it takes the brain only twelve milliseconds to react to danger, producing a mixture of chemicals that prepares the body to have an appropriate response to danger.

The trouble comes when a person finds him or herself affected by chronic irrational fear, causing disturbances such as panic and social anxiety. These disturbances occur because of an imbalance in the neurotransmitter chemicals that the brain produces. This discovery has led researchers to recommend medications that regulate the production of these neurotransmitters to combat chronic fear. The complication lies in the fact that these medicines can keep us in a calm, impassive state, even when we are facing danger, like when we are in the way of rapidly moving cars.

If danger is the result of chemicals produced by the brain, pleasure and love are as well. These chemical reactions are not only necessary, they are healthy. Fearful reactions are inversely proportional to experiences. In cases where the brain continues to overproduce chemicals despite the repetition of a learned experience, medicines can help, although in truth they only mask the problem. The source of this imbalance lies in the fact that no opposing emotions exist to repel the feelings of fear.

The physical (chemical) reactions are determined by the emotional resources, which respond to spiritual fortification. The reason why God said so many times in His Word "Do not fear" is that He alone can provide the spiritual authority to safely confront all fears.

For Laughs

I heard a story about a young girl who woke up at night during a thunderstorm. The lightning bathed the house in light, and the thunderclaps made it shake on its foundations. The girl ran to her parents' room, trembling with fear. She hid underneath the covers and shielded herself in her father's strong arms. She asked him, "Father, what's all that noise? Why does it sound so loud?" Wanting to calm her, the father thought for a moment and said, "My love, that is the voice of God, talking to His creation." After considering her father's answer for a minute, the girl replied, "Can't someone tell God to be quiet 'cause down here on Earth we're trying to sleep?"

Reflection

1. Can I identify with some of the phobias or fears mentioned in this chapter? What am I afraid of?

2. Which circumstances or factors in my life or surroundings provoke a fear or phobia in me?

3. Could I call it a healthy, rational fear or a harmful fear?

4. Were there experiences in my childhood that could have affected me?

5. Is my "alarm system" working properly? If not, what resources do I have at hand to make it return to normal?

6. Am I reacting properly to my fears? Am I facing up to them, or am I self-destructing with other things that harm me?

7. In what ways can I begin to face my fears, phobias, and anxieties?

8. Do I need professional help?

9. Who could serve as a good advisor to me?

10. Do I need to make peace with the Lord? How can I achieve this?

Prayer

Heavenly Father, God our Creator, I recognize the existence in my life of situations that I cannot resolve on my own, and for this reason I put everything in Your hands. I surrender to You all the adverse and negative circumstances that paralyze me. Please forgive my mistakes and help me walk freely and courageously. Help me erase my fears and free myself of my doubts. You are my strength and I know that with You I have no need to fear.

CHAPTER THREE

The Positive Side
of Fear

Fear has its uses, but cowardice does not.
Perhaps I will not put my hands in the mouth
of a serpent,
But looking at one should not fill me with fear.
The problem is that many times we die before
Death comes for us.

—Mahatma Gandhi

A wealthy man was looking to hire a chauffeur. He placed an ad in the local newspaper, and at the designated time, those who aspired to the position began arriving. One by one they entered to be interviewed. His interview was short and consisted of a sole question: "If we are driving on a high and winding road, how close to the precipice could you drive without feeling fear or worry?" Each interviewee had a different, dramatic answer. One said: "Oh, I think I could drive calmly within about six feet of the precipice without feeling nervous." Another answered: "In my case, I believe I could drive peacefully a yard from the precipice without being nervous or uneasy." With each person interviewed, it seemed they could go nearer and nearer the edge. One said he could be within mere inches and not be worried. After listening to many of them tell him how they could show off with a car alongside a precipice, a slightly older man appeared. When the man asked him the same question, the chauffeur's reply took him by surprise and pleased him greatly. His answer was as follows: "Honestly, sir, if I find myself on a steep highway, I try to do everything I can to stay as far away from the edge as possible. I don't try to see how close to it I can get, because I don't want to put my life or yours in danger by trying to drive too close to something that hazardous." He got the job.

Fear has its positive side: It keeps us away from the precipices of life and safe from whatever danger may come from driving too near the edge. In life, it's not about trying to see how close to disaster we can stay, but to do everything in our power to stay as far away from it as possible.

I was four years old when I read the story of Mary Poppins, the nanny who had a special flying umbrella. In the story, Mary Poppins could open it up and travel easily to anywhere in the world. I remember being fascinated by the book's drawings. There was one that showed Mary with her open umbrella, floating in the air with her suitcase in hand. On the bottom were houses and buildings and Miss Poppins had a sublime smile that radiated peace and joy. I imagine that if we could travel everywhere in this fashion, we'd have a similar smile on our faces.

One spring day, it hit me that maybe I, too, could be like Mary Poppins. My mom had an umbrella like Miss Poppins's and I began looking for it among her things. In those days, my siblings and I lived alone with my mother, who had been widowed a couple of years before. A while later, we would celebrate the arrival of our new stepfather (whom we called Dad), but he had not yet appeared and my siblings and I lived—how shall I say?—a little more "freely" than usual.

I announced to my siblings and cousins that they would witness a great event: I was going to fly with my mom's umbrella! I almost immediately had an audience on hand to applaud my great endeavor as I went up on the roof to look for a good launching spot. I remember choosing a spot below which there was a bit of green lawn to cushion my fall, just in case. With great pomp and circumstance I announced that they were about to witness something historic, and I invited them to get ready to see "the great Marcos Witt," a mere four years old, hurl himself off the first story of his house, with his mother's magic umbrella.

What follows is a little blurry in my memory. Obviously, I remember the fall and the pain in my right leg. I also remember the guffaws of my "public" and the sound of my wounded pride. But apart from that, I don't remember much, except for crawling all over the lawn, waiting for the pain in my leg to subside. Thank God, nothing serious happened to me. The situation had the potential to be much more disastrous than it was. What I noticed most was that Miss Poppins and my mom bought their umbrellas in very different places. Obviously, the one Mary Poppins bought was much better than my mother's.

A small but interesting side note: I hid the umbrella behind the main seat of my mom's pickup truck. It stayed there for many months before she noticed it. It was only when she decided to sell the truck, and gave it a good cleaning inside and out, that she discovered the famous umbrella, in very different shape from what it should have been: all the spokes pointed upward instead of down.

What I lacked at that age was a little more "healthy" fear to be able to know I'd gotten myself into a big problem. Healthy fear helps us establish parameters in various areas: 1. Health parameters, 2. Safety parameters, and 3. Happiness parameters.

HEALTH PARAMETERS

Healthy fear marks off parameters for us that assist us in living better lives. It is not the paralyzing type of fear, nor the suffocating kind that many people experience, but rather a healthy, normal fear that urges us to make good decisions and avoid bad habits. For example, knowing with scientific certainty that smoking tobacco causes cancer has forced the tobacco companies to put a warning on each box of tobacco products. In this way, consumers are alerted and cannot claim that no one warned them. Later, we came to find out that secondhand smoke, which we all breathe when we are near a person who is smoking, has the same negative effect as smoking a cigarette yourself. As a result, many public places are designated as smoking or nonsmoking. These are good parameters of health.

Everyone has to make decisions with respect to health, and healthy fear helps in this process. For example, being a person who sings professionally, I have to take certain measures to protect my voice at all costs. I never drink anything cold right after a concert, while my voice is still warm. I never begin a concert or public presentation without first doing exercises to warm up my voice. I do everything possible to sleep six to eight hours a night, and I avoid cigarette smoke, no matter what, since it affects me greatly. You must be thinking, What a fussy person. But healthy fear makes me take all possible measures to prevent the loss of my voice. There is nothing worse than opening your mouth to sing and have nothing come out. That has happened to me only two or three times and it is a truly horrible feeling. That moment of panic is my impetus to maintain the healthy parameters necessary to keep my voice in optimal shape.

Healthy fear can help us live longer, more satisfying lives. If we have problems with our coronary arteries, for example, it would be a good idea to have a healthy fear of french fries, hamburgers, Mexican tacos, and other foods that could harm our bodies. We should also try to inculcate a respectable fear of the couch and the TV's remote control, and instead go out for a walk or play some type of sport. Imagine a sign in the TV room of your home, with a black skull and crossbones and large red letters that read SAY NO TO THE RE-MOTE CONTROL. Perhaps that would help establish healthy parameters for your body. If we have a problem in this area of our lives, we should do what-ever it takes to promote good health. This is one of the positive sides of fear.

We all know people who lived their entire lives ignoring the warning signs their bodies sent, people who are now no more than fond memories of friends gone by. One of my old friends abused drugs so much throughout his life that he died at age thirty-two, leaving behind a young widow with two beautiful children. His heart simply couldn't take any more. He had abused his body so badly that one fine day his heart stopped working. A true shame. However, he had many opportunities to respect the signals his body was sending him. His doctors had told him to do so, his wife and family tried to help him understand. Not even his children could get him to change his lifestyle. Instead of having a healthy fear, he threw caution to the wind.

SAFETY PARAMETERS

Safety is another aspect of healthy fear. Traffic lights exist to keep traffic flowing and to minimize accidents as much as possible. When we see a red sign that says STOP, it's telling us it would be a good idea to stop moving. People who don't have a healthy fear with regard to traffic signs and signals are only looking for trouble. How many times have we seen individuals who think they are above obeying traffic signals, who end their lives and the lives of others simply because they don't have a healthy fear of them? Unfortunately, this is very common among young people. Recent studies demonstrate that the part of our brain that develops a healthy fear of danger isn't totally developed until we are twenty-five years old.

Dr. Jay Giedd, of the National Institute of Mental Health, has dedicated more than thirteen years to the study of the infant, child, and adolescent brain. The initial results of his research are yielding extraordinary evidence that helps us understand why children and adolescents do certain things and make certain decisions. It is now understood that the last part of the brain to develop is the part that controls critical analysis, the part that helps us make good decisions and calculates the risks associated with our actions. This study helps us understand why a disproportionate percentage of youths are involved in automobile accidents each year, and why so many young people succumb to excessive use of alcohol and drugs. Quite simply, their ability to gauge healthy fear has not yet developed.

Every day, life itself helps us to establish the safety parameters we need for living. When we were children, our mothers told us, "Don't touch the stove—it's hot." How many times has a young child, even right after his mom has told him this, go directly to the stove and put his finger in the flame? Perhaps if she hadn't said it, the child wouldn't even have noticed the stove. Why are we this way? It seems like we want to stick our fingers in the fire to prove it to ourselves, instead of accepting someone else's safety parameters. The good news is that most of us do obey new parameters. For example, after my "flight" with my mother's umbrella, I never tried to fly with an umbrella again. It took me one time to realize that I had to have a healthy fear of that.

Years later, I would become a pilot and command my own small airplane for thousands of miles of flight. However, my instructors had inculcated in me a healthy fear so deep that each time I took the plane up, I made a rigorous and detailed inspection of the aircraft to assure myself that everything was in good shape. There is a saying among pilots that goes: "It's better to be on land wishing to be in the air than in the air wishing to be on land." Many times I had to suspend a flight due to outside circumstances. If the weather was bad, if there was a mechanical failure, a problem with the engine, anything that could endanger the lives of the people who were about to board, that was reason enough to cancel the trip and look for another mode of transportation. This is healthy fear. Safety parameters. We all need them.

HAPPINESS PARAMETERS

God has given us the pleasure in life to be surrounded by persons who love and support us. People who believe in us. You and I should have a healthy fear of and respect for these people so that our trust not only continues, but grows. Many people who don't weigh the consequences of their actions make irrational decisions about their relationships, and cause horrible damage to their spouses, children, friends, parents, co-workers, and others. We should all have a healthy fear to help us establish proper parameters that govern our relationships.

With great sadness, the entire world witnessed the lack of healthy fear that former president Bill Clinton demonstrated in exposing himself, his family, and the whole nation to shame, simply by not having established certain personal parameters in his sexual life. It's unfortunate that this great statesman and politician will forever be associated with the name of this young woman even though, in truth, as a politician, his successes are far more impressive. All that because of not having a healthy fear, for making fun of the parameters of a good relationship, and for laughing in the face of moral values.

It would be easy to point a finger at everyone who has made mistakes of this nature and find ourselves somehow justified in passing judgment on them. But what of ourselves? Have we established firm boundaries in our own lives? Do we believe we are above failing? Do we think we are exempt from any of these situations? He who believes that, is closer to failing than he can even imagine. "If you think you are standing firm, be careful that you do not fall" (1 Corinthians 10:12). To have enduring relationships, we need to have good boundaries.

In your friendships: Are you a good friend? Are you there for your friends in their moment of need? Have you shown yourself to be loyal even when circumstances haven't been adequate or favorable? Have you given your friend the benefit of the doubt when people have told you gossip about him or her? Have you applied the golden rule, "Do unto others as you would have others do unto you"? In their worst moments, will you be one of the first people your friends would call?

In your family: Are you a good father? A good mother? A good son? A good daughter? Does an atmosphere of affection and harmony generally reign in your home? Does one sense an atmosphere of support, blessing, and affirmation there? Do you listen to your children with the same intensity with which you listen to your best friends? Are your children free to give their opinions and speak aloud at home, even when in disagreement with what you may think? Is there a feeling of respect for others' ideas, even when theirs may be very different from your own?

In your work: Are you worth what they pay you for your job? Do you do all you can? Have you taken measure of your level of enthusiasm? Do you put in a full day's work? Are you giving it your all, creatively? Are you honest and upright in all of your dealings? If you are the boss, do your employees like you, or are you exasperating? Are you worthy of their respect? Do you listen to them with the same intensity with which you listen to the "experts" in your industry? Do you ask them often how you could be a better boss? Do you celebrate your co-workers' victories and give them credit when due? Are you always searching for ways in which your co-workers can excel?

Another happiness parameter is living within the law as determined by those who govern our countries. The Bible says that the law is for those who are without law (1 Timothy 1:9). If every one of us had a healthy fear of the law, we would never find ourselves with the unpleasant necessity of going before a court of justice or making the acquaintance of a prison cell. If we have healthy fear, we would all obey the rules that govern the terms of the financial, business, personal, relational, governmental, and all other aspects of life. It's not hard. It's a matter of principles. We need only establish the appropriate principles in our personal lives and live according to them. It's the best way to avoid mistakes. It's that simple. A long time ago I discovered that the principles that Jesus Christ Our Lord teaches are more than manifest; they are indispensable for enjoying a complete life, full of happiness and peace.

I call this section "Happiness Parameters" because by having a healthy fear in the realm of relationships, we will live much more happily. When we break these parameters, we are breaking some of the most important parameters in our lives. We must be careful to establish strong relational bonds, knowing that when we have destroyed a relationship by not having a healthy fear, we are not only affecting a great many people, but, most of all we are affecting ourselves.

A Great Example of a Bad Example

Samson was born with a special God-given mission. He had been chosen to be a judge in his land and to help his people free themselves from the oppressive hand of their archenemies, the Philistines. Samson's famous and disproportionate power lay in the vows he made to the Lord. As long as he upheld his part of the promise, God upheld His. However, we begin to see certain traits in Samson from an early age that make us doubt the seriousness of his commitment. He got mixed up in a lot of activities that minimized the importance of his calling, he used his great God-given gift for personal effect, he did not know how to control his passions, he made fun of others, and he came to resemble one of those little boys, ridiculously spoiled by their rich parents, who has never wanted for anything in life. After reading only a little of his story, we find out that he is a man sufficiently lacking in character and overly devoted to his unbridled passions. Samson had the same failing as do many men: women.

His enormous mistakes with the ladies were not enough to help him put a healthy fear into his relationships with members of the opposite sex or to establish happiness parameters in his personal life. Quite the opposite. He lived such an empty lifestyle that each day he was more immoderate, without realizing that every time he allowed himself to engage in certain activities, he was closer to veering totally off course—a great example of a bad example. He made a mockery of his pact with God, his people, his precious God-given gift, his nature, friends, wife, and position as judge of his people. Samson never stopped to consider the consequences.

One day he met his match: the famous Delilah. She alone would bring him to his knees. With flattery, tricks, and fraud, Delilah succeeded in persuading Samson to confide the hidden source of his secret strength. It lay in a vow he'd made to the Lord that included not cutting his hair. Once she latched on to this information, Delilah grabbed a pair of scissors and cut his mane, leaving him completely weak and vulnerable to enemy attack. After he lost his powers, the Philistines came and defeated Samson in this, his final battle. Delilah was the one responsible for the fact that forever after, the story of Samson would be told with great sadness. Sadness, because it is the story of wasted potential, a moment not seized, glory trampled.

I once read that what we do not overcome will one day overcome us. This was definitely the case with Samson. When he least expected it, he confided in the wrong person and is now remembered by all mankind as the strong man who was conquered by a weak woman. Samson reacted and salvaged a bit of his dignity when he demolished the Philistines' main temple and when, in one day, he killed more of his enemies than during all other times combined. However, that paled in comparison to the sadness of the rest of his story. What's more, he was buried among the same rubble he caused, surrounded by those who hated him, all because of not establishing adequate parameters in his personal life.

What will your story be? Take a pause after completing this

chapter, go over the list of the most important people in your life, and make sure all is in order. Whatever relationships need to be fixed must be fixed while we still have these people close to us. If we have been changing boundaries or personal limits, this would be a good time to look them over and make sure we return to a healthy fear, and establish sufficiently strong parameters of health, safety, and happiness to assure us that we can successfully enjoy our relationships. We will not end up like Samson, buried amid the ruins of our own making. We will learn restraint, to contain our passions, and have a measure of respectful fear in all areas of our lives.

Reflection

1. How far away from disaster do I usually like to be?

2. Do I have a balanced, healthy fear?

3. What parameters of health, safety, and happiness am I not following in my life?

4. What am I doing to promote a healthy fear and to maintain good health?

5. Am I abiding by the instructions that guarantee my safety?

6. Am I showing respect for and a healthy fear of the people who love, support, and believe in me?

7. Am I establishing good boundaries to maintain lasting relationships?

8. Am I demonstrating a healthy fear of the law?

For Laughs

Two thieves entered the house of a millionaire. Posted on the door they found a sign that read BEWARE OF DOG. One of the thieves, the cowardly one, said to the other, "Hey, did you see the sign?"

The other answered, "Don't pay it any attention. Most people put those up to scare off thieves like us, so move away and go in the back door."

The thief obediently went around back, where he found a satellite dish, and returned to the front entrance frightened and trembling. The other thief saw him and asked, "What happened, did you see the dog?"

To which he responded, "Not the dog, but his dinner plate."

Prayer

Father, free me of all bonds and all sins that are causing me harm; protect me from all evil that comes my way. Help me maintain a healthy fear of all the things that endanger me; help me make good decisions, avoid bad habits, weigh the risks of my actions, control my impulses, and show respect for and healthy fear of the people who love, support, and believe in me. I want to live beneath Your shelter and exist for You alone. Thank You because I know that if I dwell in Your shadow, You will promise to free me from all danger and sickness and keep me safe.

CHAPTER FOUR

Do It! . . .
Even If You're Afraid

Let's put our fears behind us.

—SIMÓN BOLÍVAR

There have been very few times in my life when, in an instant, I nearly lost it. I almost always overcome the predicament I find myself in. I face challenges and valiantly confront them. I confess there have been many times when I wondered why I had to see a certain agreement through to completion, but once I became involved in the task, I bravely stuck with it. It's a vital part of my nature.

Nevertheless, I can name a couple of occasions when the moment was so grand and full of commitment that I felt truly intimidated by being in that place at that time. No doubt, the one I remember most is the time I was invited to the White House by President George W. Bush to participate in an important event for North American Hispanics. Specifically, I'd been asked to do two things: open the session with a prayer and follow it up with a song. When the invitation arrived, I felt honored to receive such a distinction and readily accepted.

Miriam and I had been invited to the White House once before, when the president brought together several of the country's prominent Hispanic leaders to announce a new political initiative benefiting the Latino community. It was a memorable occasion for us; few people have the privilege of walking through the historic hallways of that powerful mansion. That first time, during the reception after the president's speech, Miriam and I enjoyed the appetizers served on special White House plates, drank soft drinks in fine glasses, and felt very elegant and privileged to have been two of the one hundred fifty lucky few invited that day. However, that time they hadn't invited me to be *on* the program. We said hello to a few acquaintances, made a few new ones, and had our photos snapped in some of the beautiful reception rooms. I never imagined that less than one year later, they would invite me to return. Only this time, I would participate as a central figure. This moment almost threw me for a loop.

The meeting took place in the East Room of the White House, the same place where so many historic events have taken place. This is where they stood vigil over President John F. Kennedy after he was assassinated and where Richard M. Nixon's farewell took place after he was the only president in the history of the United States to have resigned. The East Room has accommodated many press conferences and important announcements, including President Bush's and Tony Blair's speeches after the events of September 11, 2001.

To this particular gathering, they had invited many senators, ambassadors of different Latin American countries, well-known athletes, journalists, also business owners and influential people from around the world. Obviously, in the first row was President Bush and the First Lady, Laura Bush. Myrka Dellanos, a host of the Univisión channel, had been invited to host the event, and when I came to take the podium, during the audience's applause, I climbed onto the small dais and looked out upon those assembled. Until that point, everything had gone fine. In my hands was the prayer I had written and submitted more than two weeks earlier. I invited everyone to join me in prayer. I have never had any problems speaking, and in a way, addressing myself to the Lord in the presence of all those dignitaries was therapeutic for me. It helped me remember that the only one greater than all of them was the One whom I was addressing at that moment. When I finished the convocation, they moved me to another part of the platform to sing. This new spot was opposite the president and no more than five feet from where I had been standing. For the occasion, I had selected a song based on Psalm 121, which has been a great blessing to countless persons, myself included. I figured that the best thing I could sing in this important place, in front of such special people, was not a song of my own, but the very Word of the Lord, since it is the only eternal Word.

The song's rather lengthy instrumental intro began. While the music played, I said a few words of introduction that I had practiced very carefully days before. After I spoke, the musical intro continued and the moment to start singing had not yet arrived. In that very moment it happened! I looked around, saw all those important people, the president and the First Lady looking at me with rapt attention, that historical room, and suddenly I felt that the moment was much bigger than myself. I fought to maintain my composure, making sure not to let the smile fade from my lips. I thought I would not be able to make it through that challenge. I had never before felt such sudden, absolute panic. It lasted a very short time—a matter of seconds—but it seemed like an eternity. My heart beat rapidly, my mouth grew dry, and my breathing accelerated. I knew that this wasn't the time to waver, so I quickly took inventory of the situation and pulled myself together. I thought, They invited me here because I can be here. They believed in me enough to put me on this dais, and I will not let them down! I can go through with this! I seized the moment and thought to myself: "You won't defeat me! I will enjoy this moment, I will succeed, and my grandchildren and great-grandchildren will know that I sang in the White House and I did so with honor, dignity, and consummate professionalism."

The rest of the story is good. I got through that moment of anguish, and I began to make eye contact with every person in the room as I sang the benediction. I pronounced that blessing on the lives of all those present, the country, the White House, and the president. I did it with authority and professionalism; I didn't miss a single note, and by the end of the song, while sustaining the last note (a very high, climactic one), the audience began to applaud before I even finished.

This was one of those times when we often have to do things in spite of our fear. If I had allowed my fear to win out and let that solemn moment defeat me, perhaps I would have left that day with the experience of having *been* in the White House, but not of having performed with grace.

ACTION DISPELS FEAR

Inaction produces doubt and fear. Action produces confidence and bravery. If you want to conquer fear, don't sit in your house thinking about it. Get out and start acting.

—DALE CARNEGIE

Action contains a powerful element. Most of the time when we fear doing something, it becomes less scary than we had imagined once we start doing it. Inaction produces a lot of fear. That indecisive state creates a mental and psychological paralysis that will keep us from doing many of the things we want to do. People who always doubt themselves, analyze every angle, and play that psychological game of "And what if this happens? . . . Or what if that happens? . . ." never enjoy life. They don't have time to act because they spend all their time doubting, fearing, and questioning. We must understand that most things in life aren't achieved through chance or luck, but because we set a goal. That is the key: move toward the goal. We can only reach it one step at a time, and when we least expect it, we will have arrived.

Jesus' apostles crossed the Sea of Galilee one night after a long day of work. Peter found himself in the same boat as all the disciples. Peter was a man of action; he liked to be where things were happening. When we think of him, we picture an intelligent man full of energy and enthusiasm. On that occasion, when Jesus remained behind and the disciples had taken the oars of the boat to arrive at their next destination, the Master decided to catch up with them a little later. Since there were no other boats available, He walked on the water until He caught up with his disciples. When they saw Him from afar, some in the boat were frightened. Obviously, for who had ever seen Jesus walk on water? It was natural to be frightened. From far away, Jesus told them not to fear. He said: "Relax! It is I. Do not fear." To which Peter replied: "Lord, if it is you, command me to come to where you stand on the water." Then Jesus told him: "Come," and Peter got down out of the boat and walked on water in the direction of Jesus (Matthew 14:29). In that instant, any one of the disciples could have done what only Peter did. Any of the others could have asked permission, like Peter, to walk on water together with the Lord. But they didn't. We don't know if it was because they were too afraid or if there could have been some other reason why they didn't think like Peter. The thing is, instead of being invaded by fear or doubt, Peter saw a great opportunity. He had faith and vision. Instead of letting the moment defeat him or letting "fate" dictate the outcome, Peter took control.

Surely, when Saint Peter the Apostle stepped out of the boat, the others must have thought he had gone crazy. They couldn't believe what they saw. Being the close group of friends that they were, I daresay more than one of them voiced his "opinion" about why Peter shouldn't do this. I imagine everyone had his thoughts on the subject, and there may have been those who wanted to stop him. Thomas, for example. I imagine he heard Peter asking Jesus for permission to walk on water and he suddenly thought: Okay, I really *doubt* Peter is going to succeed. We can only imagine what Judas Iscariot must have been thinking, but what I don't doubt is that everyone had an opinion, because what Peter had asked to do was outside the realm of "normal" or "acceptable." He had dared to dream beyond what man had ever dreamed of before. As a result of faith mixed with action, Peter became the only person in history, besides Jesus, who could say he walked on water.

How many experiences, activities, achievements, and opportunities have you missed simply because you were not ready to take action? Perhaps you've dreamed a long time of starting a new business. You should have begun taking active steps toward this dream. First, by reading everything that has been written about this kind of business, asking others about their experiences opening businesses, designing the logo for your business. All of these steps will eliminate the fear of starting something new. Maybe you've thought about learning a new language. You should have taken steps toward this dream, by at least looking for a book, or an audio or video educational guide. If you don't have the money to buy this material, the act of asking about prices gives you the goal of knowing how much money you need. That is at least a positive action toward breaking down the fear of learning a new language. Possibly you've wanted to travel to a new country, visit new cultures, and have new experiences. You need to be taking steps toward this dream: asking about airfares, looking up information about the city you want to visit, learning all you can about its people, customs, language. These actions will begin to break the fear.

I remember my first day of flight instruction, in 1995. I had always wanted to fly. Finally, one day I took action and went to a small airport where there was a school of aviation, with the goal of inquiring about prices, schedules, requirements, and so on. I went merely to get some information, but I returned home registered as a student. I would be lying if I said I wasn't nervous. After I'd finished the first class, my shirt was totally soaked with sweat. I didn't stop sweating intensely until after one or two months of instruction. Five months later, I got my pilot's license and flew for several more years, accumulating more than two thousand hours flying as pilot-in-command. After so many hours in the air, it has become second nature to me. I don't think about how scared I was that first day of classes, but of how moved I feel when I fly. The action I took the day I inquired about classes resulted in achieving one of the biggest dreams of my life. The same will happen to you. Action dispels fear, and you will get closer to your life's goals and dreams. What Robert Schuller said is very true: "It is better to do something imperfectly than to do nothing perfectly."

What You Say Is What You'll Do

Words are important. They mold our thoughts, shape our judgment, and build our future. It is crucial that we choose our words well. It is equally important to choose well that which we permit to enter our heads and hearts. What enters is what will come out. "Of the heart's abundance, the mouth speaks" (Matthew 12:34). "How a man thinks in his heart, so he is" (Proverbs 23:7). For this reason, we need to be careful to let only good things enter our minds and hearts. We cannot grant access to negative, pessimistic, or destructive thoughts, because our thoughts produce our actions. Our actions produce our future. If we always speak in negative words, we will have negative outcomes. If we are always forecasting our destruction, that is what will happen. If we are always predicting our misery, or declaring our misfortune, that is exactly what we'll get. We get what we say, and what we say is what we get.

Words have a powerful way of affecting our future. For example, if I hear myself say, "I am a successful man . . . I know that today will go well for me," my mind, my heart, and my emotions are more likely to believe that this will happen because they heard me say so. If

I make positive words part of my vocabulary, my faith will be activity and faith activates actions.

Words that are negative, fearful, or full of doubt only reinforce those pessimistic and dark forces. If that is the style of our vocabulary, that will also be the style of our lives. We need to ask God to help us erase our life's negative thoughts, so that they are not converted into words that will determine our fates. We need to adopt a vocabulary full of faith and optimism, and believe that things will turn out.

The bravest action one can take when one doesn't feel brave is to profess courage and then act accordingly.

—CORRA HARRIS

One of the most effective ways to destroy the fear in our lives is by speaking to ourselves out loud. In this way our words penetrate the depths of our being to reprogram the fear that dwells there. When our interior being listens to words of reaffirmation and courage, the fears begin to lose their power. When we least expect it, the thoughts of faith, victory, and triumph win.

I remember when I was taking some advanced aviation courses. After receiving my pilot's license, I took a fairly complicated course to get a special license to fly by instruments. This is the type of flight that lets a pilot fly in the clouds without becoming disoriented. This course is so intense that it requires absolute concentration and adherence to an endless number of complicated rules. The rules have to do with following certain flight patterns, tuning in certain radio frequencies, and following the needles and compasses on the cockpit's flight panel. Some of these are very complicated exercises that require the pilot to do three, four, or even five things at the same time. I will never forget the feeling in my head during those first classes. I felt as if my brain would explode from all of the information it was having to store in such a short time. The more the lessons advanced, the more complicated they became. They were intense days, because learning the maneuvers well was a matter of life or death. My instructor reminded me of this every day. In some of the more complicated maneuvers, he showed me a very interesting tactic: speak out loud. My instructor told me that if I could memorize some of the key words of the maneuver, I would never forget that important part of it. In fact, he explained, if I find myself feeling doubt or fear, insecure about where I was or what follows next in the exercise's sequence, I should speak out loud to remind my brain of what happened already and what comes next. What's more, he told me, speaking aloud has the very positive psychological effect of making you feel that you're not alone. I later realized how right my instructor was.

One night on a flight from Houston, Texas, to Monterrey, Mexico, I used the technique my instructor had shown me. We took off a little late from Houston, and I knew that part of our flight would be after sundown. That didn't worry me since I'd flown many hours at night. In fact, flying at night is a delight since the air is much more stable, there is less turbulence, and one experiences the serene beauty of the stars above and the city lights passing below. What I did not know was that the weather conditions in Monterrey would worsen before our arrival. With a half hour to go before landing, we entered a rain cloud. Thank the Lord, there was no thunderstorm or lightning. In my little airplane, a twin engine Cessna 310, there was a dim red light to read the maps and the flight information at night. There are lists with the preestablished routes that we have to follow with absolute precision and concentration. If we followed the instructions correctly, we would not collide with a hill outside of Monterrey or encounter any other mishap. The key is to follow the preassigned routes faithfully.

Suddenly the air traffic controller radioed to tell me that he had noticed that I was more than five miles outside the preestablished route (printed on the lists I had in my lap at that moment and that I should have been following without deviation). I answered immediately that I would check why I had gone so far off route. I automatically consulted my books, my radios, my lists, the needles I needed to follow, but I could not find the error. This was all happening at night, inside a cloud, with the noise of the rain slapping against our plane and with the dim, little red light that barely allowed me to see my lists and instructions. My heart began beating quickly. My hands began to sweat.

Our speed at that moment was approximately 205 miles per hour. The flight controller's insistence made me nervous, and I knew that I had to remedy this problem very quickly. We were only five minutes away from starting our descent to land. Five minutes at the controls of an airplane that is going that fast can seem like hours. I knew from our altitude that we were out of danger, in terms of the hills, but it seemed like an eternity until I discovered where I had made a mistake.

Suddenly, I remembered my instructor's advice: "Talk out loud." I began by getting my attention loudly: "How did you end up off track? You don't fly that way. You're a good pilot, so fly this plane!" Then I spoke all the flight instructions aloud, one by one, revising all the radio frequencies I had to tune to, to fly in that particular pattern. The mere act of hearing my voice in the cabin of the airplane had a calming effect. My heart stopped racing, my hands stopped sweating a bit, and I realized that I was going to be okay. Once I calmed down, I began to think clearly, my fear began to dissipate, and it was then that I discovered the error that had made me deviate from the route. A simple mistake, but very important to correct. Within two or three minutes

To fight fear, you have to act. To make fear grow, just wait, postpone, do nothing.

—D. J. SCHWARTZ

of beginning to speak out loud, I had found and corrected the error. I communicated my problem to the air traffic controller and he gave me new instructions to return me to the correct flight pattern. In seconds, everything was fixed.

I knew I had no option but to keep flying the plane, so I did, fear and all. The power of my audible words was the key to locating the error, calming my nerves, and giving me back the tranquillity I needed to be able to land the small plane. Some of the passengers were frightened to hear me talking out loud; they didn't know what had happened. I regret that I passed some of my fear on to them, but the result of my speaking out loud was good because we all landed safe and sound.

We don't just repeat something over and over or talk out loud like it's some kind of mantra or magic spell. We do it to activate our faith. For human beings, faith is a powerful thing. Jesus Christ said: "For he who believes . . . all things are possible" (Mark 9:23). If we can believe something, we can attain it. If we doubt, that is what we will attain—doubt. We will attain that which we say, and that is why it's so important to be careful about what comes out of our mouths. We should speak words full of faith, optimism, and positivism. Do things even though you fear them. Fling yourself out to walk on water like Saint Peter the Apostle.

If It's Possible, Take This Cup from Me

At a time of great anguish, we see Jesus in the Garden of Gethsemane praying all night long. He is fighting a great battle. He knows that the only way to bring salvation to humanity is by following the plan that the Father entrusted Him with: to dedicate Himself as a perfect sacrifice, in repayment for all the sins of the world. However, being human, Jesus knew that what awaited Him would be extremely difficult. His divine nature did not suffer, but His human nature did. Jesus understood that to be hung on the Calvary Cross would be the most intense and horrible pain that, as a human, He would have to endure.

I have neither the authority nor the daring to speculate if Jesus was "afraid" on this occasion or not. It's possible that He battled those emotions. The Bible teaches that He was a man just like the rest of us and that He felt the same things we have all felt. Therefore, I do believe I have the authority to say that, at some point in His life, Jesus felt fear. I don't know if this narrative, in Gethsemane, was one of those occasions or not, but it might have been. What we do know is that it was a moment of such intensity that He sweated drops of blood. Perspiring blood is a condition of extreme stress.

Upon speaking with His Heavenly Father, He said: "Father, if possible, take this cup from me; what is more, do not my will, but yours" (Matthew 26:39). In effect, He was saying "If there is any other way to pay for humanity's salvation, that would be good. But if this is the only way to achieve it, I don't want You to do my bidding, I want You to do yours. I am ready to suffer this martyrdom, this sacrifice, this pain so long as it fulfills Your eternal wish." This is acting with bravery, determination, faith, and valor. This is how we should act, as well. I can't be sure that in this exact case Jesus felt "fear," but I can assure you that His example of confronting one of the most difficult moments of His life and facing it with courage and surrender is one more reason that He is, for me, one of life's greatest heroes.

His example has served me well in my periods of suffering and weakness. It has helped me to know that I, too, in spite of being human, can face difficult times and come out victorious. His example allows me have the power to do what I have to do despite fear, doubt, or apprehension. His ability to face that cruel cross has helped me overcome lesser challenges, for I have never had a test as great as the one He withstood. Nevertheless, He bore His cross to Calvary with dignity and surrendered all for love of humanity. What a great example!

In life, we will find ourselves in many situations in which we'll have no other option but to go forward. We'll have to do certain things despite our fear. We'll have to act with faith and courage no matter how difficult it is to ignore our apprehensions. This is part of the decision to live. Do it—even if you are afraid!

A Success Story: My friend Cristina de Hasbun worked for many years as a flight attendant for an airline of her native El Salvador. One time she flew in a 767 to Los Angeles, with a stop in Guatemala. When the plane made that stop, everything seemed fine: the plane had landed, and they were just waiting to come to a complete halt so that all 215 passengers could deplane. Once on the landing strip, the captain, as usual, put the engines in reverse to reduce the speed. But strangely enough, the airplane didn't slow down.

Cristina recounts that in a matter of seconds, the airplane began to vibrate, causing the light system to activate and deactivate repeatedly, generating great panic. At the end of the runway was a ravine, and since the plane still had 30,000 pounds of fuel left, a terrible explosion seemed inevitable.

Suddenly, the airplane made a U-turn and headed toward a hill, but to make matters worse, the door to the cockpit opened and a cloud of dust blocked the pilot's visibility. "We're going to die! We don't even know where we're going, and we're all going to die. The pilots can't even tell where the airplane is headed," said Cristina, who found herself seated right behind the cockpit.

The plane continued on its way, out of the pilot's control. One of the wings carrying the fuel managed to avoid a security booth that was the same height as the wing. The other wing was releasing fuel from an opening about six inches in diameter. At precisely the spot where the airplane passed, and right below this wing, a group of people were having a cookout. Miraculously, instead of setting off an explosion, the fuel put out the cooking fire.

After a few desperate minutes, the aircraft began to slow down three feet from a high-tension wire that threatened to hit the vertical stabilizer located on top of the airplane, where the rudder is. If this had made contact, a fire surely would have broken out. People were screaming desperately, searching for an exit. The plane finally came to a halt in front of a tree, a branch of which entered the cockpit and stopped mere inches from piercing the pilot's throat. The plane's back doors then opened so they could inflate the evacuation chutes. But to add to the desperation, another branch pierced one of the chutes and it exploded. Even so, Cristina, together with all the attendants, was able to evacuate the passengers via one chute in the record time of fifty-nine seconds.

"Thank God that no one died and no one was seriously hurt, although the plane was left totally useless and would never again be flown," Cristina de Hasbun tells us today, fourteen years after the incident.

Because of the accident, Cristina was incapacitated for a month, affected not only by a spinal injury but by a great fear of landing.

"During the entire month, everyone asked me, 'Are you going to fly again?' " Cristina recounts. "My husband told me, 'Better you should give it up; don't fly again.' But I told myself, 'If I don't fly again, my fear of landing will never go away.' "

When the month was up, Cristina had to confront her fear, as she needed to return to work.

"During every landing, I asked, 'And what if it happens again? What if the brakes don't work again? What if there's another accident? And what if today we really do die?' I had a lot of negative thoughts when we landed. I continued to feel this way for several weeks, all the while flying with fear, with the same rapidly beating heart. But I knew I couldn't stop flying because if I ran away from the fear, it was going to rule my life."

For about six more months, Cristina experienced the same symptoms. She kept doing exactly what she feared until her fear disappeared completely. Cristina explains how one day a close friend, who also worked for Taca Airlines as a flight attendant, came to her and said something that changed her life and helped her overcome her fear.

"The Bible verse that probably left a mark on my heart was from Psalm 121: God will guard my coming and going from today on and forever more," Cristina added. "That verse was what sustained me after returning to flying. To this day, it's a phrase that destroys whatever fear tries to knock on my heart's door. And the time came when the fear disappeared and I could walk and work. I worked six more years for the same airline."

The story of Cristina de Hasbun is indisputably another story of success. She was able to *do what she was afraid of doing*; she faced her fear and was able to surmount it. In the same way you, too, will succeed, once you decide to face your biggest fears. So, do it—even though you're afraid!

For God did not give us a spirit of fear, but a spirit of power, love, and self-discipline."

—2 TIMOTHY 1:7

Like my friend Cristina, you and I have to overcome our fears and move forward. Take action to succeed. Put your mouth to work in your favor, and when you least expect it, that fear will be a distant memory. You will begin to live in a new and different way: with vigor, enthusiasm, and filled with faith.

For Laughs

A mountain climber found himself in serious trouble. After having ascended to a fairly high point on the mountain, his foot slipped on a rough spot, causing him to fall several hundred meters. As he was heading toward the base, he caught hold of the trunk of an old tree sticking out of the side of the mountain. A few minutes after recovering from his fear, he began to scream, "Help! Help! Is there anyone there who can help me? Help!" Silence.

He looked all around to see what he could do. Again he screamed: "Is there anyone there who can help me? Help!" Nothing. After many terrified screams, he suddenly heard a deep, booming voice: "I can help you. Just let go of that branch."

"Who are you?" asked the mountain climber.

"I am the Lord," the voice answered. "I can help you, but you have to let go of the branch."

The mountain climber thought deeply for several minutes, weighing his options. He suddenly yelled, "Isn't there anyone else there who can help me?"

Reflection

1. Am I bravely dealing with my commitments and facing my challenges?

2. Am I intimidated by my commitments and afraid to follow through?

3. Am I missing the chance to enjoy life by constantly analyzing it?

4. Which goals have I still not met because of my fears?

5. What actions can I begin to take to dispel these fears and achieve my dreams?

6. What types of words are part of my vocabulary? Are my words full of faith and optimism?

7. What kinds of thoughts am I letting enter my mind?

8. Do I have an optimistic attitude toward my goals?

9. Think of optimistic phrases you can say out loud to dispel your fears, and then do so.

Prayer

Dear God, help me face my commitments and defeat all fear, insecurity, and intimidation. Take away my mental and psychological paralysis and help me act in pursuit of my dreams. Change my way of speaking, make my vocabulary always full of faith, optimism, and positive words. Take away all pessimistic thoughts that may invade my mind and all negative feelings that reach my heart. Thank You, for You have promised me that if I believe, everything is possible.

CHAPTER FIVE

Don't Let It Defeat You

Don't be afraid to go into the unknown,
For where there is risk, there is also reward.

—LORI HARD

In 1989, I had the inspiration to bring together musicians, composers, arrangers, singers, producers, and sound engineers for an outstanding event of learning, inspiration, and motivation that I named Music '89. For the event's headquarters, I chose the city of Guadalajara, in western Mexico. It was an extremely ambitious dream. I never imagined that this would be the start of a movement that would shortly flood Latin America.

During the early days of organizing the event, we traveled to Guadalajara to meet with executives of the hotel and convention center that would serve as our headquarters. The hotel, an imposing skyscraper in an accessible area of the city, had a main reception hall that held about two thousand people. We thought that if all went well, we could dream of having nearly fifteen hundred participants at the evening meetings.

A few days after that trip, my secretary, Gloria Quiñones, told me that the official contract for the engagement had arrived and that we needed to sign it that same afternoon. When I heard her words, I had a hollow feeling in my stomach, not because it was bad news, but because it was a whole new avenue for me, and the seriousness of a signed contract made clear the weight of my decision. Additionally, the hotel asked us to guarantee a certain number of guests, along with other sundry details that seem unimportant now but which at the time seemed like an enormous, new mountain to scale. If we didn't occupy the number of rooms that the hotel required, we would still have to pay for them. This involved great sums of money, which neither I personally nor our company, CanZion Productions, had. I didn't even want to think about what would happen if we failed. The weight of the decision fell squarely on my shoulders.

I left for my home to eat lunch and to speak with Miriam about all of this; I wanted to know her feelings. Over the years I have found that my wife is very good at critical decisions, and her advice is invaluable to me. For this historic decision, as for so many others in my life, I needed her advice. The more we talked it over, the more my faith grew and the less I feared faring badly with the hotel or not having enough money to cover all the agreements. I returned to the office with the document in hand, signed it, and sent it to Guadalajara that same afternoon, thus beginning a new, exciting stage of our life.

It was a miracle of God that that first conference was so successful. We hadn't had the slightest idea about how to organize a national event. Nevertheless, this is a story about going forward in spite of what others say or foresee.

The lesson of that signature has been this: Had I allowed fear to take control on the day that I had to sign the contract, we never would have celebrated Music '89 nor been blessed with touching the thousands of lives that these events have reached. When I signed that paper, I didn't know that this simple act would establish a gathering that would inspire a number of outstanding events. This marked an unprecedented step in the growing history of Christian music in Latin America. In just a short time, events would pop up in every country on the continent, many of which were inspired by and modeled after those we originally organized in Mexico. What a single decision can potentially achieve is much greater than we can even imagine.

How many things have we failed to do because we were afraid to take the risk? How many victories have we failed to enjoy because we were invaded by fear and couldn't finish what we started? How many dreams have been forgotten because the dreamer didn't have the perseverance to go on believing? Surely we all have many unrealized dreams because we lacked the courage to dare. We must walk with daring and faith, believing we can achieve what we set out to do. The day I signed and returned the contract to Guadalajara, I did it with fear and trembling, knowing that if things turned out badly, I alone would have to answer to the hotel. My hand shook when I picked up the pen to sign my name. Fear was totally present; I merely rose above it and won. But that doesn't mean that fear hasn't visited me on several occasions since then.

Thousands of questions passed through my mind during those days: What if people don't respond? What if the day of the event comes and no one shows up? How am I going to repay these tens of thousands of dollars? What if this? What if that? Thank God, it went well for us. On the opening day, there were so many people that we overflowed the central auditorium. At the last minute, we had to find an adjoining hall to accommodate the extra people who watched it on the video screens we hastily installed. After using up more than one hundred twenty of its rooms, the hotel simply ran out of quarters and had to start calling other hotels to find available rooms. I will never forget the absolute chaos that reigned in the hotel lobby as we registered the hundreds of people who had shown up in Guadalajara, coming from every corner of the country to spend those three marvelous days with us.

What would have become of this story had I not signed that paper? We will never know, thank the Lord, but I can imagine that things would not have ended up the same way. An action so simple as signing my name on a contract touched thousands of people.

What is stopping you? Which fear has you paralyzed, unable to make the decisions necessary to realize your dreams? Maybe you're afraid of failure. You're afraid of going into too much debt. Don't give up. Act, unmotivated by fear, but rather by the moving thought of the victory you'll have if you run the risk. Don't give up. Persevere, overcome your fears and realize your dreams.

FEAR OF REJECTION

Since a young age, I had a problem with wetting my bed every night, because my bladder was too small for my body. My parents tried every means to help me, but with no luck. This condition lasted throughout my childhood, into adolescence and young adulthood. I can't begin to recount all the completely embarrassing situations I endured because of it. I wet the beds at my cousins', aunts', grandparents', friends', hotels, etc. I was the butt of jokes from insensitive people who thought they were funny. For me, the joke turned into a huge weapon of rejection that bothered me for many years. I regarded the jokes as deeply personal, and my self-esteem suffered. For a long time, I had a poor self-image and a big inferiority complex. I thought the only thing I knew how to do well was wet the bed. I thought the whole world knew about my problem and thus wouldn't accept me.

Now, after several years, I understand that I exaggerated the problem, but in my young mind, there was no bigger problem. That feeling of inferiority and rejection paralyzed me in many areas. I was afraid of being rejected or teased. For example, many times when I was asked to sleep over at a friend's house, I didn't because of my fear of wetting the bed. My mind processed it this way: After they found out I wet the bed, they would be disgusted with me, then they would mock me. They would never invite me to their house again and would tell all our school friends what happened and none of them would invite me over after that. So the simplest thing was to not accept their invitation. Case closed.

Many people live their whole lives this way. Their imaginations run wild, and they write the end of their own imaginary movie based on their fears, complexes, and phobias. Don't be one of them. If for any reason you have to face rejection, you can learn something from the experience. We can get better. We can make rejection a good friend. At least we know that God will never abandon us. Arm yourself with bravery, face rejection, and don't let it defeat you. Remember the words of the Apostle Paul, who wrote in Corinthians: "God chose the lowly of this world and the despised things—and the things that are not—to nullify the things that are" (1 Corinthians 1:28).

Fear of Failure

I think this has always been my greatest fear. For years I've struggled with the thought that someday I'll arrive at one of my concerts and there will be no audience. I remember the first time I organized a concert in the beautiful city of Cancún, Mexico. Although I had never given a concert in Cancún, we had decent expectations. But on the day we arrived in the city, I found out that they had rented a baseball stadium for the event, one that held around ten thousand people. I panicked. I thought: Why did they decide to rent such a huge stadium in a tourist city, where people want to go to the beach, not listen to someone sing?

I struggled with this all afternoon before the concert, preparing myself psychologically to arrive at the baseball stadium and not see more than a few of those loyal fans who always show up, no matter what. As we neared the baseball park, we encountered a tremendous traffic jam. That night they not only filled the arena, but there were people seated on the walls around it, watching through the bars on the doors, and from the rooftops of surrounding houses. This was a great lesson for me.

I always thought that the day I arrived at an auditorium to play and there was no one there waiting for my concert would be the worst day of my life. Now I can say that it was not. How can I say this? Because it happened to me. With total sincerity I can affirm that there are many worse things in life. It was also a good exercise for my ego. It helped me to keep remembering that everything we have is thanks to the divine kindness of God Our Father and that without Him, we can do nothing. If we always keep Him first in our lives, we can go forward, and failure is not something we'll fear. What's more, we know that if we have Him, we have everything. "If God is for us, who can be against us?" (Romans 8:31). On the other hand, remember that what the world calls "success" or "failure" may be very different from how the Lord defines them. For example, the day that I arrived at the concert where there was no audience was a success for me. I passed a beautiful test that reminded me that I am a product of His Divine Grace. It was a positive experience because I didn't get depressed or feel bad. My musicians and I had a great time, laughing and enjoying the moment and knowing that even though, for whatever reason, no one came, our worth didn't lie in the size of the audience but in the size of God's love for us. That day was not a failure. It enabled us to learn valuable things about ourselves by dealing with the situation. Even though it might seem like a failure in others' eyes, you and I can see it differently. Everything depends on our point of view. Don't let your fear of failure win out over you.

Fear of What Others Will Say

We all suffer when we know that people have a bad opinion of us. Words can wound us and be painful. We all wish for others to hold us in high esteem. But in reality, that will never be. There will always be those who have their defined opinions of us, and no amount of work will change what they think. No matter how much we want it, we can't make everyone think well of us. Once and for all, decide that you will not let the fear of others' opinions keep you from realizing your dreams. Don't fear what others will say.

One of the greatest discoveries of my life has been recognizing that no matter how conscientious I am, or how hard I try to make people think well of me, in the end, they'll think what they want to think. If we worry about changing our hairstyle, there will be those who think it looks absurd. Even though we think we're dressed in the latest style, there will surely be someone who thinks we're badly dressed. If we wear the most fashionable shoes or not, if we have the right brand of wristwatch or not, it won't change the fact that there are people who will think whatever they want of us, regardless. So let's eliminate the fear of what others will say, because one way or another, they'll say something. If we always try to live our lives according to what others say or think, we'll live a mediocre, miserable existence, without achieving our own dreams and goals.

Fear of Criticism

The first cousin of What Others Will Say is criticism. It's hard to take criticism from other people, especially when it's not well intentioned. The criticism that's easiest to dismiss comes from people who don't even know us or our intentions, let alone our motivations. They are far outside our lives and don't even try to get closer, probably for fear of discovering that their analysis of us is incorrect. Normally, that kind of criticism comes, as Miguel Angel Ruiz Obregoso says, from "people whose only known occupation is their sharp tongue." If we let this kind of criticism paralyze us, we need to find professional help. Really, we should not care about what other people think. It can't help us at all.

There is another, more painful level of criticism. It's the kind that comes from people who do know us and our dreams and visions, and who have examined the motivation in our hearts. And who, despite all this, choose to criticize us. That hurts a lot. I imagine we've all been exposed to that type of criticism, although I wouldn't wish it on my worst enemy. It is the most cutting, wounding, painful, and paralyzing kind. The only thing we can do to protect ourselves against this type of criticism is to know that it will come and mentally prepare ourselves to face it when it does. It helps to talk to someone who has already faced this kind of situation; it will help us to share their experience and gain the maturity needed to deal with this type of criticism. For as painful as it may be, we should not allow fear of this criticism to keep us from going forward.

A man who lacks judgment derides his neighbor, but a man of understanding holds his tongue.

—PROVERBS 11:12

There are several steps we can take each time we face criticism. First, consider the source. In other words, whom does it come from? If it's from someone who loves us, who appreciates us, who is interested in us, then it's a good source. On the other hand, if it's from someone who hates us, who repels us, who simply wants to attack us, then it's not a good source. However, if it's someone who doesn't even know us, then it's a questionable source. Second, weigh the words spoken. Meaning, in what spirit were they said? In the spirit of helping us, or in the spirit of merely attacking us? We should try to weigh that spirit and analyze the tone of voice and their intention. Was it premeditated or just spontaneous? If it came in good spirit, we should listen to the criticism, as it can become our best friend if we let it. If, on the other hand, it comes with venom, all it will do is hurt us. Or maybe the criticism was neither well meant nor ill meant, but simply the result of someone saying the first thing that came to their mind. We can discard this type of criticism accordingly. After having considered the source and then having weighed the spirit in which the criticism was made, then we can decide to embrace or reject the criticism. If we embrace it—because it came from a good source and was well meant—that criticism can become a real ally toward helping us become better people. If it's something that came from a bad source—poorly intentioned and wishing us harm—we need to reject it. If we embrace poison, we will poison ourselves. For this reason, if we want to receive positive criticism, we should always try to give positive criticism. As Psalm 19:14 says: "May the words of my mouth and the meditation of my heart be acceptable in your sight . . ."

The last kind of criticism should be the easiest, even though it can also hurt to receive it: constructive criticism. This is the type of criticism found on the lips of people who love us and who wisely know how to balance their friendship and their commitment to us. Every one of us should have the blessed fortune to have a few people in our lives who speak to us with frankness and clarity, who help us become better people. If we make their comments our friends, they can help us overcome any deficiencies in our character, personality, profession, or vocation. We must embrace constructive criticism, learn from it, and let it work its medicine on us. If we take it in a negative way, we are the only ones who lose.

I would like to underline the difference between constructive and destructive criticism: one helps, and the other doesn't. Helpful criticism will come with answers; its opposite tells us what's wrong, then leaves us to fix it however we can. Constructive criticism presents solutions, and is spoken in a tone of voice that demonstrates the positive intentions of the person giving it. Now, there is also criticism spoken with bad intent but which has at its base a truth that can help us. I can filter out all the bad and be left with no more than the good and be better. There is a verse in the Bible that says: Examine everything. Hold on to the good (1 Thessalonians 5:21). We should not let ourselves be overcome by any kind of criticism, whether it was well or ill intended. We should keep moving forward. We are much bigger than the criticisms tossed at us!

I am blessed that my wife, Miriam, and I enjoy a relationship filled with a great deal of communication. Since we were boyfriend and girlfriend, we have delighted in this blessing. After twenty years of marriage, we continue enjoying it. In fact, the more time that passes, the more we speak on a great variety of subjects. One of my greatest pleasures is listening to Miriam comment about my teachings, writings, songs, or communiqués. She always affords me an interesting, fresh, and different perspective. Almost every Sunday, with very few exceptions, we have long conversations about the

Sunday sermon that I present to the Christian congregation that I lead in Houston, Texas. These conversations have made me a better communicator. They help me think as a theologian. They enhance my ability to formulate and set forth my arguments. Her comments, almost all of which are positive, have been central to helping me better deliver the truths of God and life. What would I do if I had a wife who withheld what she was thinking? I would not have the richness of her mind. I would not enjoy her creativity or her ideas. Thank the Lord that a long time ago I found out that constructive criticism from the mouths of people who love me and who are committed to me, is one of the best resources that God, in His grace, has given me.

There are also many times when disagreements arise between the two of us, and people ask how I resolve them. I believe many things have no solution; many disagreements will simply exist. There's a saying that goes: "Respect has no quarrel with anyone," and I respect Miriam's opinions as much as she respects mine. So if we know we don't agree on something that's not crucial—for example, if I like salsa music and she doesn't—we can disagree, but we respect each other. On the other hand, when we have disagreements on crucial matters, the best thing for us to do is talk. We do this often, and many times they are long debates, which at times become complicated and the conversation gets intense. However, by talking we reach a common accord. Today, Miriam and I have no crucial disagreements in our life.

FEAR OF SUCCESS

It may sound strange, but many people never move forward because they fear success. They know that success means having to make decisions, accept more responsibility, and solve more problems, so they prefer to live their lives without these additional pressures. Sad, but true! There are some who don't want to accept the social pressure that they may receive from their friends and family for having a more successful life. They don't want to answer questions that are sometimes embarrassing or difficult to answer. For example, isn't there always a curious buddy who asks odd questions like, "So, how much did you pay for that trip, man?" Gulp. They swallow hard and don't want to get into the discussion that will ensue once the buddy with less money hears what his best friend just spent on a trip that might seem frivolous. Some people would rather not have money than face this kind of situation. Many reach the threshold of success and quit because the burden seems too great. They prefer to live in the status quo of what others think than achieve their own dreams.

Success is going from failure to failure with great enthusiasm.

— MARK TWAIN

I remember when I boarded an Aeroméxico flight from the city of Torreón to Hermosillo, another city in the north of Mexico. Back then, I was not as well known as I am now, yet many people recognized me. At the time, I traveled almost exclusively via Aeroméxico.

After one becomes a frequent flyer, the airlines give you certain privileges, like a free upgrade to first class. I'd received one that day between Torreón and Hermosillo and was quite glad, since it was not a short flight.

After settling into my seat, I began to read. I then felt someone touch me on the arm and ask if I was Marcos Witt. I looked at the person and said yes with a wide smile, only to find the troubled face of a tall, thin, young woman with a bag slung over her shoulder. She made a disapproving sound, turned away, and continued toward the back of the plane. A few minutes after takeoff, the flight attendant brought me a piece of paper, explaining that it came from a passenger at the rear of the plane. You guessed it! Our friend: the "bothered" one.

In her letter, the young lady attacked me severely for traveling in first class. She told me she found it impossible to believe I could sit there totally free from guilt, while many of the people who attended my concerts and bought my music didn't even have enough money to pay for food. She complained bitterly, using Bible verses that cited Jesus when He says: "Whoever wants to be great among you, must be a servant" (Mark 10:43), among others. Her letter was very accusatory and aggressive, and did not contain even a pinch of desire to understand my side of the story. She had reached her own conclusions.

Her letter hit me very hard. It didn't matter that I was unjustly attacked. It hurt because I have always been devoted to others and sensitive to their needs, especially those who are humble. It was among them that my own beginnings lie. Her attack made me feel so bad that I immediately stopped enjoying that first-class seat. I felt guilty. I felt bad. I wrote her a note explaining why I was seated in first class, that I hadn't "squandered" my money on that luxury, and I asked if she'd do me the favor of praying for me. I never heard from her, but her poison had hurt me. Even though it had nothing to do with me, I let that person's opinion keep me from enjoying a benefit I was given simply for being a frequent flyer. Every time I had the same upgrade, I found myself seated in the aisle, staring at the floor, without looking at the faces of the passengers who passed by me, almost pained to be seated there. How absurd! That was fear of success. Fear of enjoying the benefits bestowed on me as a result of my perseverance and persistence. The most incredible part is that someone is going to enjoy it, so why shouldn't it be me? I can assure you that I was able to overcome this fear of success a good while back, thank God.

But how was I able to overcome the fear of success? First, I know the truth and that makes me free, as Jesus Christ said. I know the truth of who I am, of my life and my environment, and I can be at ease knowing that the blessings that God gives me come because He, in His grace, is loving and favorable to us. Understanding this truth has set me free from the criticism of people who do not know this truth. The majority of the people who criticize us do so because they don't know our reality. Second, I understand that everybody has his own opinion, and that is his right. I can't force people to think what I want them to think. That has given me peace in time to enjoy my God-given success.

We should not fear success simply because there are people

who don't think we deserve it. We should be excellent at what we do, diligent in carrying out our tasks, persevering in meeting our objectives to reach our dreams, and unconcerned about others' opinions. In the end they'll have them anyway, no matter what we do. Whether they're good or bad should not influence us. Remember: Those who truly love us and are in relationships with us will be the people who will give us a point of view that may possibly help us (constructive criticism), but the opinions of those who neither know us nor anything about our reality, are garbage that we can discard without giving another thought.

One fine day, months later, it became clear to me that the young lady's issue with me, that morning on the Aeroméxico flight, was her problem, not mine. I could finally put that letter in the closed archive of my mind and go forward with no guilt. In fact, now when it's my turn to receive an upgrade to first class and people are boarding the plane, I look them in the eyes. It doesn't bother me that they know I fly first class, because I know the truth and that frees me. I hope never again to be in a mind frame where another person's opinion keeps me from enjoying the benefits I've worked many years to achieve. Same for you.

Fear of Being Imperfect

No one's perfect, although many try to achieve perfection. The Bible says that there is no one righteous, not even one (Romans 3:12); Jesus alone is perfect. The most you and I can aspire to is to keep fighting against the negative parts of our character, polishing our personality, and becoming the most like Our Lord Jesus as we can. Dr. Cristina Ruíz de Coloma wrote a book called *Dare to Not Be Perfect*, which, among other things, speaks of the problems that can arise when people strive for absolute perfection in their lives. As mere mortals, we can never hope to achieve absolute perfection. It's important to have a desire to improve continually, but when this desire takes us to a rigid perfectionism, we stop enjoying life, friends, and successes as we constantly seek out all the mistakes we and others make. Dr. Ruíz de Coloma writes: "The rigid perfectionist suffers problems, feels frustrated and sad, irritable and insecure, and lives poorly because he repeats tasks several times trying to do them better. He feels a profound anxiety over what he considers an imperfection, and will keep trying to find an immediate solution to it." In other words, they lead frustrated lives because they measure everything against an impossible yardstick. Because of whatever they may have disliked, they ruin the whole experience. This is an unhealthy state.

I love Dr. Ruíz de Coloma's idea: Dare to Not Be Perfect. The day we understand that we are not perfect and therefore make mistakes will be a very happy day in our lives. We can enjoy the reality that not everything we do will turn out well, but we can still enjoy it.

We can enjoy the effort that went into the planning, executing, and developing the project and its results. If everything did not turn out perfectly, at least we can say that we gave it our best effort. Trying to be perfect is, in effect, setting ourselves up for failure. In the words of Dr. Ruiz: "To look for perfection is somehow equivalent to failing, because you can never reach the stated objective." Don't be afraid of imperfection. Don't be defeated by perfectionism.

FEAR OF BEING "MADE A FOOL OF"

In chapter 2, we talked about common fears and phobias. One of the most common fears is that of being made a fool. It is called social phobia. Many of us have kept ourselves from achieving our big dreams for fear of turning into public laughingstocks. Yet if we never run the risk, we can never achieve many of the things of which we've dreamed. We need to ask the Lord to help us to defeat this fear so it doesn't keep us from achieving our dreams. If it is something even more deeply rooted in your life, look for help, but don't let this fear keep you from being successful.

One of the antidotes to this fear is to allow people to laugh at you. I believe this is one of the healthiest characteristics that anyone can possess. We don't take ourselves so seriously that we haven't the ability to recognize when it's a good time to laugh at something we may have said or done. Practice doing this—look at yourself in the mirror and laugh at yourself. Tell yourself things that help you have a less serious attitude about yourself. Those who take themselves so seriously never enjoy life. Laugh, enjoy—life is fun. In the moment you suddenly do something ridiculous, this attitude will help you to laugh and move on instead of hiding in a dark corner, bitter for the rest of your life. Don't become bitter; laugh at yourself. Don't hide; laugh at yourself. Don't be sorry; laugh at yourself.

"But," you say, "the whole world laughed at me." So refocus your thoughts in the following way: "How great that I had the chance to give people a break and a moment of happiness at my expense. How great that I had the chance to bring a bit of joy to people's hearts." Instead of being resentful or embittered, turn whatever ridiculous thing you did into something positive. You will come out much better, I promise you. Don't be afraid of being a laughingstock. We all are at one time or another in our lives.

An Extraordinary Example

One of the people who surprised me most when I studied his life was Joseph the Dreamer. We find his biography in the Bible, in the Book of Genesis, chapters 37 to 50. It's a story of perseverance in the face of some of the biggest obstacles an individual may have ever faced. It's a story of absolute determination, of survival, and of clinging to a dream. It's a story that should inspire you and me not to quit in the middle of the journey, but to keep moving until we attain our dream.

Joseph didn't allow anything to stop him, despite the fact that some of his obstacles were bigger than those most of us have experienced. Perhaps it is true that some reader has been through similar things, but I assure you that he is the exception and not the rule. Joseph's brothers ridiculed him. Not only didn't they believe in his dreams, they insulted and made fun of them. Imagine how Joseph must have felt, and yet he didn't give up.

One day, his brothers schemed against him and put him in a pit. They took the multicolored coat his father had made him, killed a sheep, and bathed his cape in blood so they could tell their father that he had been devoured by a lion. A few of his brothers even thought of killing him. I cannot imagine the degree of frustration that these brothers felt toward Joseph for them to make such radical and mean-spirited decisions. What kind of damage had Joseph's dreams caused them to merit this type of response? Obviously, their actions and decisions show us something about the meanness, bad attitudes, and the poor state of the hearts that ruled those boys.

Finally, one of his brothers convinced the rest of them that, instead of killing him, it would make better business to sell him. In this way, Joseph arrived in Egypt as a slave, far from his home, his father, and his family, but still with his dreams. He went from being the favored child in his home to becoming a slave in a faraway land. Everything was different, yet he wasn't defeated. He continued conquering his surroundings and attaining the best for himself.

Joseph was such a good worker that after a short time on the job, he would be promoted to boss. In the home of Potiphar, his owner, Joseph became the chief steward because he was such an extraordinary person. He never let the rejection, jokes, criticism, or anything else keep him from doing his best at whatever he tried his hand. This is mastering one's circumstances, dominating ourselves instead of letting ourselves be dominated. But Joseph's story doesn't end with him being the chief steward in Potiphar's house, but with his once again having to face calumny, lies, and deception. As it turned out, Potiphar's wife had unseemly designs on young Joseph and made up a slanderous story when he rejected her advances. From having held the position of chief steward, Joseph once again found himself ridiculed and abandoned, only this time he was in an Egyptian prison, far from all whom he loved. Alone, enslaved, slandered, rejected, deceived, and resigned to the misery of imprisonment—anyone else would have given up and forgotten his dreams. But not Joseph.

In a short while, the jailer had given him work. He was such a remarkable person that he turned every opportunity into an occasion to move forward. Instead of lamenting his stay in prison, Joseph saw how he could improve his surroundings. He looked for what he could do to occupy his time, better his talents, and increase his knowledge. Joseph never let his circumstances change him. Rather, he always changed his circumstances. Against all odds, he became the jail's administrator. Now, that is winning and not giving up!

Like all of us, Joseph could have let the rejection, the lies, the betrayal, the slander, the hate, the jealousy, and the bitterness that people felt toward him keep him from achieving his dreams. But he didn't. Instead of letting these negative forces dominate him, he overcame them and was successful. And how successful! With the passing of time, it became known that there was an unusual young man in the prison who possessed extraordinary gifts. When the pharaoh

sent for him, Joseph, without knowing it, was positioned to experience the most extraordinary time of his life. All those years of rejection, hatred, bitterness, and lies were about to end in the most
important position a man in those times could have. Second only to
the pharaoh, Joseph became the person who rescued not only the
Egyptian people from great starvation, but also many other surrounding countries, turning himself into one of the greatest examples
of stewardship and leadership that history has ever known. What
was his secret? Don't let circumstances defeat you. Keep on overcoming them with your unshakeable faith, absolute devotion, and
total determination, never mind the size of the challenge.

This example should help us adopt an attitude of overcoming
adverse circumstances. We all have to deal with them. We all have to
confront them. Unfortunately, we don't all respond positively. Some
of us, when confronted with rejection, failure, slander, or criticism,
don't let it make us stronger. We flee to a dark corner and let bitterness possess our thoughts. Rather than pouring our creativity into a
positive force that will carry us to positive conclusions, some of us
pour our creativity into a series of vindictive thoughts that merely
plunge us deeper into the dizzying darkness of total slavery. Don't be
one of those people! Arise! Go on! Overcome all those adverse situations that life has brought you. Do not give up.

No matter the scale of your fear, there is help. The Lord is on
your side. His Holy Spirit has been sent to help us go forward. There
are people who surround us, who love us, and who are ready to do
anything to see us move forward. Think of these people and don't
give in to your fears. If your fear is deeply rooted or profound, seek

help. It won't be hard to find a professional counselor who can help you untangle your thoughts so you can triumph.

In the end, Joseph realized all his dreams—to a much greater degree than he had imagined and definitely to the surprise of all his brothers, who lived long enough to see all their little brother's dreams come true. They had made the mistake of categorizing Joseph as crazy, without knowing that he was a persistent dreamer, with an excellent character, devoted to the idea that his circumstances should serve him, and not the other way around. You and I will do the same! We will overcome all our fears, get them under our control, and go forward in life, victorious in our dreams and triumphant in every one of our longings. With this kind of determination, together with God's help, there is no way to fail.

For Laughs

At midnight a thief broke into a house to rob it. He entered through a window, and when he got inside he heard a voice call out from the darkness: "Jesus is watching you!"

The thief became frightened and stopped. Then when he saw that nothing happened, he continued. Once again the voice called out: "Jesus is watching you!"

The frightened thief turned on the light and saw that the voice belonged to a parrot in a cage, and the thief said to him: "Oh, what a fright you gave me! What's your name, little parrot?"

And the parrot responded: "My name is Peter."

"Peter is a strange name for a parrot."

To which the parrot replied: "Not as strange as the name Jesus is for a Doberman."

Reflection

1. Do risks, impediments, and challenges intimidate me?

2. How many dreams have I failed to reach because of fear?

3. What should I do to stop questioning myself every time I am presented with an opportunity to achieve success?

4. Which fear is intimidating and paralyzing me?

5. Do I fear failure or success?

6. Do I feel inferior and fear rejection?

7. Do I fear ridicule, criticism, what others say, being imperfect, or being a laughingstock?

8. What things can I begin to learn from bad experiences, rejection, and the criticism I've received?

9. How can I begin to turn my failures into victories?

Prayer

Lord, help me to walk with faith, believing I can achieve all that I propose. Give me the courage to pay the price of risk. I want to begin to take actions on behalf of my dreams. Help me make wise decisions, assume my responsibilities and commitments, and resolve problems properly. I ask You not to let me give up. Help me be indifferent to all that does not edify or profit me. Take away all discouragement. Show me how to turn my failures into great victories. Thank You for strengthening me and promising me that with You, all things are possible.

CHAPTER SIX

Perfect Love Fights Fear

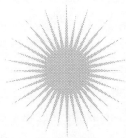

Courage is contagious.
When a brave man adopts a firm stance,
the spines of others are stiffened.

—BILLY GRAHAM

I was raised in the city of Durango, in Durango state in northern Mexico. My parents didn't have much money, but they always tried hard to provide us with the best they could. My childhood is full of lovely memories of family outings, days in the country, trips to visit our relatives, and other activities that my parents, in their free moments, always strove to give us. They very much believed that family bonds are strengthened by spending free time together. Almost every week, they planned some type of activity so we could all be together. Without a doubt, our favorite trip was going to visit the beautiful city of Mazatlán, located exactly where the huge Pacific Ocean converges with the Sea of Cortés. This is something we did at least once a year. We traveled a twisty highway full of curves, on a journey of about 186 miles and six hours, passing through the great western Sierra Madres with their impressive valleys, peaks, and the famous Devil's Spine—a band of mountains that looks much like a backbone. I imagine it earned its name because of how dangerous this section of highway was, and because of how many people had experienced accidents there. I didn't like the trip because I always got carsick. Less than two hours after leaving the city of Durango, I was already vomiting. But I very much liked arriving. Once in Mazatlán, we loved being at the beach, enjoying the sun and the sand.

As a young man, my dad had been in the navy and knew how to swim well, and he taught us to bodysurf. My three brothers and I loved this activity. Every day, we eagerly prepared to return to the beach, jump into the waves, and keep on improving our bodysurfing skills. My brother Jerry is two years older than I, much taller, and was without a doubt the best surfer of the three boys. My mom didn't swim. She stayed at the edge of the sea, reading, resting, or playing with my little sisters in the sand or water. Once in a while, she'd stick her toes in the water, but I never saw her go in deeper than her knees.

I will never forget the trip when I celebrated my tenth birthday. For my birthday present, my parents gave me my first watch. The second unforgettable thing was a lemon meringue pie that my father bought to celebrate my birthday. It tasted so awful that we ended up throwing it in the garbage, and to this day, the whole family hasn't stopped laughing out loud whenever we remember that disgusting lemon pie. But what I most remember was the incomparable love that my dad showed me in an extraordinary act of bravery, faith, and courage.

One morning we went down to the beach to continue our bodysurfing adventure. My brothers and I waited anxiously until my dad was ready to go out in the waves with us. When we finally went into the water, the bottom of the sea seemed different. It was a series of undulating valleys that ran parallel to the beach, spaced about one or two yards apart, and no more than eighteen inches deep. Upon crossing them, we ended up once again in shallow water. When we had crossed two or three of these "valleys" we felt confident enough to keep walking deeper into the ocean, where we found the good, big waves that we wanted to surf. The only problem was that suddenly the ocean floor betrayed us. Thinking we had entered just another "valley," my big brother and I realized, too late, that the floor was gone. Within seconds we found ourselves in deep water; the sea roared around us. When I saw what was happening, I de-

spaired. Despite knowing how to swim well, in the anxiety of the
moment I made the bad decision to fight the tide. I wasn't able to swim
for more than a few seconds before I started to feel tired. The terror of
being in such danger flooded me even more and I began to scream:
"Dad! Dad! Help!" My older brother also yelled for him. When my
father realized we were in trouble, he came to us as quickly as he
could. He began shoving us, first me and then my brother. Again and
again. Since Jerry was taller than me, he reached land more quickly
and began walking toward the beach. But I was in deeper trouble. I
was tired. I was more desperate. I was beating the water, and my father yelled to me to try to get on top of it, to "lay" my body in the
water instead of trying to touch bottom, as I had been doing. He kept
on pushing me, pulling me toward the shore, until finally I stepped
on firm land. I never could have done it without my dad.

I cannot describe what I felt the minute my father's hand
touched my arm, when I found myself in absolute despair that memorable morning of my life. It was the touch of steady love. It was a
touch that gave me strength, courage, and the desire to keep on fighting despite how difficult the situation seemed. My dad's love ban-
ished the fear I'd been feeling. Literally, when I felt his hand in mine,
I thought, "Everything is okay now. My dad's here. We'll get out of
this." I would not know until many years later that my father had felt
doubtful about our situation. The tide was so strong and the cross-
current pulled us so savagely that it had swept the two of us away
with a furious determination. Although he doubted our recovery,
but he decided that come what may, he would never abandon me.
When I heard him say that, I felt something that moved me in the

deepest reaches of my being: It is called love. Perfect love that drives away fear.

The world would be a much better place to live in if we all had this type of love. If every one of us had the privilege to experience in our own flesh the kind of love my dad showed me that day in the Pacific Ocean, the world would be a gentler, kinder, safer place.

The Power of Perfect Love

Before my dad came to my rescue that day at the beach, I wasn't thinking straight. I didn't control my impulses. I fought unsuccessfully against the tide. Until love arrived, I hadn't felt the security it brings. It was at that moment that my thoughts began to become reasonable. I listened to his instructions; I followed them because I had hope. I felt my father's love. In the same way, there are many people in life who wander aimlessly, living in fear, without thinking rationally, because perfect love hasn't come into their lives.

Saint John the Apostle, a disciple of Jesus and one of the persons closest to our Lord, wrote the following words: "Perfect love drives out fear" (1 John 4:18). When the writer uses the word *fear*, he is referring to the kind of insecurity that produces terror, fright, and blind fear, just like a disobedient slave feels before a whip in the hands of a cruel master. Where there is perfect love, there is no fear, because love does away with the whip. Love builds confidence. When there is love, there is no fright. Loving hands caress; they don't hit. Loving arms embrace; they don't struggle. The power of true love is immeasurable. The positive results love can have on the heart of man are incalculable. What's missing in the world to destroy fear is more perfect love.

There's another expression Saint Paul the Apostle uses when speaking to his disciple Timothy, in his second letter to him. He tells him: "God has not given us a fearful spirit, but a spirit of power, love, and good judgment." Another translation of the Bible uses the word *cowardly* instead of *fearful*. It's interesting, because fear produces cowardice, another kind of fear that paralyzes us in the face of possibilities. Through this word, the apostle wanted to encourage Timothy, since, as his teacher, it is possible that Paul had determined some of his pupil's weaknesses: timidity and fear. To teach him about the power we have by being in possession of "self-discipline," Paul wanted to encourage Timothy to discover that it was not necessary to let oneself be dominated by fear, but rather that he could dominate himself through the self-discipline that comes from being under the powerful spiritual influence of the Lord. The perfect love of God could help him have the self-discipline needed to be strong, defeat fear, and succeed in life.

God wants you and me to discover this same lesson. God wants us to know that we can live free from the spirit of fear, and walk in love, power, and free will. If we let the Lord's true love inundate our lives, we will never be the same. We will never more be slaves to fear, panic, or the frights that want to invade our lives. We can live free, thanks to the perfect love of the Lord. Fear paralyzes people. Fear is an obstacle that slows the path to being a winner and keeps us from having the dreams that God has programmed us to conquer: our promised land, the dream of our lives, the destiny for which God created us.

In the Old Testament, we find the great story of the liberation of the people of Israel. For hundreds of years, they had lived in slavery under the reign of the Egyptian pharaohs. Finally, thanks to the great liberator Moses, they could leave that situation and begin their journey to the Promised Land. For many centuries, the land had belonged to their fathers, but they lost control of it when they moved to Egypt, and now it was inhabited by their enemies. When they got close to their old homeland, the people of Israel sent twelve spies to investigate, to find out what conditions were now like, and to know what kind of enemy they would have to defeat to reclaim their land. Ten of the spies returned full of fear, paralyzed by fright, recounting things that seemed impossible obstacles. Fear became such an obstacle to them that they described the inhabitants of that land as giants that could not be defeated. They succeeded in convincing everyone that entering this land was impossible and that they should stop trying. Only two of the spies returned with sufficient faith to enter and take possession of what was theirs by God's promise and by inheritance. However, these two spies, Joshua and Caleb, didn't have enough influence to convince the others that they could take back that land. Nearly forty years would pass before the Israelites would succeed. When they entered the country, of the twelve original spies, only these two giants of the faith remained. All the rest had perished in the desert without having tasted the Promised Land, as do so many who never realize their dreams. They prefer to believe in fear and die in their personal desert than dare to believe they can take possession of what God has promised to give them: their destiny.

We all have a "promised land" that the Lord prepared for us. We must only destroy whatever fear we have, give faith a chance, and possess it. Many people have seen the realization of their dream fade away because of the fear that rules their life. Is it possible that you will not enter your promised land because of fear? It's important we understand that fear is a weapon in the hands of the enemies of our soul, used to keep us from our blessings. Don't be afraid of fear. Destroy fear; put perfect love in your life, and you will see how everything will change.

FEAR IS A LIE

It was interesting for me to learn that lions are the kings of the jungle not because of their brute strength, but because of the intelligence with which they seize their victim. The male lion partners with female lions, using his strong and terrible roar to intimidate the victim. Upon hearing the roar, the lion's victim runs in the opposite direction from where the sound came, unknowingly running toward the female lions that await ready to attack. The male lion does not kill the victim; the female lions do. The male merely roars. Nothing more. If the victim ran in the direction of the lion's roar, the male lion would be confused and it's quite likely that the victim could escape with its life. In the same way, you and I, upon hearing the roar of any "lion" in life—a difficult problem, an abandonment, a betrayal, or any other unpleasant situation—can run toward the sound of the roar, because the lion can't do anything to us. On the contrary, if we flee from the problem in a cowardly manner, rather than coming out triumphant, we will find a big trap from which there is surely no escape.

Saint Peter the Apostle wrote the following words: "Our adversary, the devil, prowls around like a roaring lion, looking for someone to devour" (1 Peter 5:8). The devil is like an old lion that only roars to try to frighten us and make us run in the opposite direction. Over there his horrible demons lie in wait to destroy us. We have to remember that the devil no longer has teeth that can bite. The only thing this poor defeated devil still has is his roar, because Jesus defeated him mightily, once and for all, on the Cross of Calvary.

I was surprised to read a study by the University of Michigan that contains the following statistics about fear:

- 60 percent of fears are baseless; they will never come true.

- 20 percent of these fears are focused on the past; what happened in the past is completely out of our control. There is no longer anything we can do about it.

- 10 percent of fears are based on such insignificant things that they will not make an important difference in our lives.

- Of the remaining 10 percent, only 4 percent to 5 percent could be considered justifiable fears.

These statistics demonstrate that we invest 95 percent of our time and energy in fears that do not produce anything positive and represent a big waste of our time. Let's give up the futile task of worrying about things that will never change or for which there's nothing more we can do. Let's instead invest our thoughts in things we can change, that are worth contemplating, and which we can do something about.

The Truth About Perfect Love

The best way to destroy a lie is by speaking the truth. The Lord said: "In love there is no fear; rather, perfect love drives out fear." (1 John 4:18). To live free from fear, we need to firmly establish the perfect love of God in our lives. It is interesting that Saint Paul the Apostle gives us the characteristics of perfect love in his first letter to the Corinthians. He writes that perfect love is: 1. Long-suffering: a word that means patient, restrained, and that knows how to wait. 2. Benevolent: true love is one that always looks for a way to give rather than receive. It is generous. 3. Without envy: jealousy and envy are two attitudes that don't fit within true love. There is simply no place for them. 4. Not boastful: in other words, humble. 5. Not vain: it has no ego. It doesn't think more highly of itself than it should. 6. Does nothing improper: it is correct. It knows restraint. It knows how to maintain good sense and control in keeping with the occasion. 7. Doesn't look out only for itself: perfect love is always making sure that the others are seen to first, that their needs are being met before its own. Later it will see to its own needs, but not without first taking care of everyone else. 8. Doesn't get irritated: it gives the benefit of the doubt to people. It looks for cordiality, getting along. 9. Does not hold a grudge: it quickly forgets wrongs committed against it. It has a short memory with regard to others' mistakes or offenses. 10. Dislikes injustice: feels genuine pain when injustice wins out. It fights for justice. 11. Enjoys truth: when truth wins out, true love has won. 12. All-suffering. 13. All-believing. 14. All-hoping. 15. All-enduring. Incredible, but true! That is the true love of the Lord. With good reason, Saint John the Apostle likened this kind of love to the love that destroys fear. If we all had more love, the world would be free of fear.

When God's perfect love lives in us, fear cannot reside there. The two cannot live together. This is why we need God's love to be a vital part of our lives. When we begin to know the nature of God, we can understand God's perfect love. Once again it is Saint John the Apostle who declares a great and eternal truth when he says: "Whoever does not love has not known God, because God is love" (1 John 4:8). By obtaining this perfect love we begin to discover the Divine nature. Not until then will fear leave our lives. Upon knowing how the Lord is, how He thinks, how He speaks, how He acts, fear will have to flee, because He is love, and His true love will rid fear from our lives.

How to Know God Better

1. The first way to know Him is through His Word. The Bible teaches us about the love of God. It is His manual of instructions for

humanity. It contains God's thoughts about us. The closer we get to His Word, the more we will know Him, how He functions, how He thinks, how He acts. The most extraordinary thing is that His advice works for leading a practical life. Obviously, He created us, so who better than He would know how our life functions in relation to the creation? That is only one of the many reasons why we need to be as close as possible to His Word.

2. We can also know Him by getting together as much as possible with His family and living with His children. As is true with many families, by getting close to the patriarch, we will get to know the family's children better, in the same way as when we get close to the Lord, we can know His family better. And as in any other family, the family of God has a little bit of everything. For example, we can be sure there are those family members who always talk in a loud voice, brag about things they never did, insult others, are extroverts, and generally noisy. By the same token, there are brothers who are patient, kind, well behaved, and gentlemanly. However they may be, they are family and one loves them like family. As we get close to the family of God, we will know more about how God treats His children, we learn mutual love and respect. It's a great experience, a great adventure that will enrich our lives.

3. Another way we can know more about God is through reading good Christian books and listening to Christian music that praises God. Why? Because they help us have a different perspective. The thoughts of other people as expressed in their works help us see God from the point of view of another person who is also con-

tinually seeking to know Him. Christian music can leave us a lot to think about, as well as elevate our spirits and hearts in praise and adoration of the Lord.

4. Another way to know the Lord is through spiritual exercises such as prayer, fasting, praise, and adoration. In the intimacy of prayer, for example, we can speak with God and tell Him our uneasiness, our dreams, our frustrations, and our quarrels. Fasting sensitizes our spirit to spiritual activity and allows us to have an ear more open to the voice of God. Praise and adoration lets us celebrate, enjoy, sing to the one we love, and enjoy an intimate communion with Him, who also comes closer to us, helping us to know Him more deeply.

By knowing Him and embracing His Divine nature, we will also embrace the love of God. Therefore, our arms will be very busy surrounding Him. Our embrace will be so strong and enclosed that fear will not be able to get in. If fear appears before us, we'll have to say to it: "Excuse me, fear, my arms are very busy holding the love of God, I cannot embrace you now, so get out of here!"

THE BLESSINGS OF PERFECT LOVE

Embracing perfect love brings enormous benefits to our lives. If I try to list them all, I will never finish. But I will make an effort to create a short list of just a few of the blessings we enjoy when we embrace the perfect love of God.

1. Confidence.

By accepting the love of the Lord, we walk confidently, with fear of no one and nothing. For example, when my wife walks at my side, her walk is confident, because she takes my arm and walks calmly. In the same way, my safety should be in the Lord, because He is my light and my salvation; whom shall I fear? "The Lord is the stronghold of my life—of whom shall I be afraid?" (Psalms 27:1).

2. Security.

Feeling safe is one of the biggest challenges in today's world. Especially in recent years, insecurity has covered the global terrain, thanks to several incidents of terrorism that have directly or indirectly affected every inhabitant of the planet. It seems that wherever we go, we feel this insecurity. However, he who embraces the perfect love of God knows that one of the promises He has made to us is to be with us, no matter where we are or where we go. The psalmist David wrote about it in this way: "The Lord is with me; I will not be afraid. What can man do to me?" (Psalms 118:6).

3. Authority.

Fear not only paralyzes us, it also removes this feeling of security, making us doubt the authority we can have in life. When one doesn't step firmly (fear), one doesn't know where to go (insecurity). But by knowing the perfect love of the Lord, personal security and authority become apparent and we can make the declarations that King David made on an occasion when he felt threatened by his enemy: "I will not fear the tens of thousands drawn up against me on every side" (Psalms 3:6). It is the same kind of authority that we who have embraced the perfect love of God can feel.

4. Happiness and joy.

The consternation that results from seeing ourselves surrounded by fear and feeling like we cannot control the panic life produces, causes us to lose our passion and happiness for life. But when we begin to know the perfect love of God, everything can change because we have the possibility to declare what the wise Solomon did when he wrote: "We will be glad and rejoice in You; we will praise Your love more than wine" (Song of Songs 1:4b). It doesn't matter what the world throws at us, we can be sure that God's perfect love will sustain us through every test and that we will be able to prevail with happiness and joy in our hearts. In fact, "The joy of the Lord gives us new strength" (Nehemiah 8:10). So it is time to enjoy ourselves, to be happy and laugh despite whatever difficulties we may be going through.

5. Satisfaction.

The great satisfaction that God's perfect love produces makes us feel complete and allows us to recognize that we want for nothing, for we have the most important thing: His perfect love. After all, feeling love brings completeness. The author of Songs of Songs experienced this same feeling when he said: "I am my beloved's and my beloved is mine" (Song of Songs 6:3). There is a great feeling of satisfaction when two people love each other.

Do not be afraid of God's perfect love. It will merely be the beginning of a life filled with satisfaction, security, authority, confidence, and happiness. If the world were full of more of God's love, fear and dread would have to flee. There would be no room for them. Remember that when we embrace the perfect love of God, we have no room to embrace anything else. Our arms will not be able to hold any other emotion. Embrace God's perfect love right now.

For Laughs

Paco and Lolita had been married thirty years. For more years than Paco could recall, Lolita awoke every night upset, shaking him awake. "Paco, I hear noises in the house. There's a thief walking around the dining room. Go see what's happening."

So Paco put on his slippers and robe and went down to the first floor to see where the noises Lolita heard were coming from. Upon finding everything in order, he went back to bed and told his wife, "My love, there's nothing there."

Year after year, the same thing happened. Finally, one night Lolita heard a noise and shook him awake again and said excitedly, "Paco, there's a thief in the house."

Like always, Paco put on his slippers and robe and went down the stairs. But unlike all the nights before, there *was* a thief checking out the furniture. Upon seeing Paco, the thief said, "Give me everything you've got!"

Paco calmly got out the china, the silverware, the

perfumes, the jewelry, and the money. When the thief was about to leave, he told Paco not to move or call the police, but Paco asked, "Mr. Thief, could you be so kind as to do me a favor?"

Intrigued by the request, the thief asked him, "What do you want?"

"Please, go upstairs for a minute and say hello to my wife. She's been waiting for you to get here for thirty years."

For Laughs

Johnny had spilled his cup of milk. He was three years old and had the motor reflexes of a child his age. But his mother's constant lessons would bear fruit one day. The child decided to clean up his own mess. He ran to the door that led to the back patio of the house, and suddenly realized it was dark outside. Fear overtook him, but he did not want to show it. When his mom saw what was happening, she told him: "Don't worry, John. Remember that Jesus is everywhere, even in the darkness." The child thought for a moment, lifted his little head up to the door, and screamed: "Jesus, if you're out there, please pass me the mop!"

Reflection

1. Am I in control of fear, or am I letting it control me?

2. What traumatic experiences have I been through that could be causing my fear?

3. What is my promised land?

4. In what way can I begin to take steps toward conquering and mastering my fear?

5. How sure am I of having God's perfect love in my life?

Prayer

Dear Lord, I entrust You with all the traumatic experiences that may have impacted my life and given me fear. Help me discover and practice power, love, and the self-control that You have bequeathed to me. I want to know You, and I wish to accomplish all You have promised me. For this reason I ask that You take all fear away from me. You are my light, my salvation, and my life's strength, therefore I have nothing to fear. Thank You because Your love casts away all my fear.

CHAPTER SEVEN

You Can See Everything Better in the Light

*I consider more valiant he who overcomes
his desires than he who conquers his enemies,
because the victory over oneself
is the most difficult kind.*

—ARISTOTLE

I completed my first recording in 1986, the same year Miriam and I were married. It was a great time of happiness that marked both our personal and professional lives. I had always dreamed of recording and finally I had achieved it. Miriam and I were surprised by the speed at which my career took off during those first few years. We hadn't expected it, we could not have foreseen it, and we surely weren't prepared for it. Within less than a year of getting married, we were crisscrossing Mexico, singing and giving conferences in an endless stream of activity. Being recently married and without the blessing of children, we put our hearts and souls into these events for several years, until our little girl Elena was one year old and Miriam decided to stay home with her. The trips were fairly destabilizing for my daughter because of the lack of routine in her young life. Miriam and I agreed that the time had come for her to say good-bye to the constant travel.

A little more than six years after recording my first project, the number of people who came to my concerts and events every year was truly surprising. My trips continued, with the same intensity as always, only my responsibilities had grown. We had founded our first business, CanZion Productions, and it was growing at a crazy rate. In one year, we experienced a growth of more than 400 percent. To be at the head of all daily decisions caused me great personal stress, and took up a lot of my time. At this point, Miriam and I had the added blessing of welcoming two of our three sons, Jonathan and Kristofer. With a growing family, career, and business, I entered into a personal crisis that would last, in one of its stages, almost six years of my life.

I didn't seek help because the progression of this crisis was so subtle and slow that I never thought it would cause me much trouble. Also, in the circles in which I moved, there wasn't much of a culture of "seeking help." It was more of an atmosphere of producing results, of "doing," of work, of performing, and of being responsible. If one had personal problems, one was expected to do the best he could to move forward. Thus, I began to sink into a state of depression that would last more than three years. This was the most difficult stage of the six years of my crisis. My depression was so great that on many occasions when I returned to my hotel room, I threw myself on the bed and cried, sometimes violently, for long periods. The strangest part of it was that many of these times, I didn't even know why I was crying. I just cried. On other occasions, I cried because of specific events that set me off, some kind of criticism from someone I cared about, some mistake I made in my program, etc. I was completely sensitive to what others said or thought about me. It didn't help that in some parts of Mexico they attacked me strongly because my music was too "contemporary" and they didn't see why I had to use certain musical instruments to express my praise of the Lord. Most of these attacks came from people who were entrenched in their thinking and were not open to a new form of expression to God. Still, their comments and judgmental spirits hurt me greatly.

One day several young people in the Christian congregation of Durango, where Miriam and I belonged, came to tell me that one of the local congregations had invited the youth to bring their Marcos

Witt cassettes (CDs were yet to be invented) because on that certain Saturday they were going to take all these cassettes and burn them. They claimed that they were inspired by the devil himself. This is the type of news I heard too often during those years of crisis. It pained me through and through. I was sinking and closing myself off more. I had a smile on my face, but my heart was weeping.

Everything came to a head around the year 1996, when I was thirty-four years old. Over the previous ten years, I had married, then experienced one of the fastest growths in the history of Latin American Christian music. I had written a new story for musicians and singers all around Latin America, having sung and spoken to millions of people in the largest stadiums and halls on the continent. But I could no longer shoulder my burden. I could not keep crying every night after the concert. I couldn't keep smiling at the whole world and ignoring the fact that my heart was breaking. I needed help. By then Miriam knew of my battle, not because I had told her but because one desperate night I came into our bedroom at home and she asked me why I was so sad. I tried to deny what she was saying, but it was no use. She insisted on an answer. I knew it was time to speak.

Thanks to God and to Miriam, who forced me to talk, I finally was open to my need for help and it was the start of a marvelous story of help, recovery, and reintegration—a story that continues to the present day, because, thank the Lord, I have understood that it isn't something that happens to us once in life, but that we need to be on constant guard against it happening again. I continue to take part in certain activities with the aim of not falling back into the state I found myself in at the end of 1996.

What was the recovery process? Bringing everything to light. That simple. With light, you can see everything better. As long as I insisted on living in the darkness of depression, pain, and anguish, I never would have recovered. I would probably still be trying to exist with a smile on the outside and pain on the inside. But it is so difficult to live that way. There is no better way to live than with absolute transparency by letting the light penetrate every part of one's life. I am convinced that there are millions who embrace fear because they haven't let the light penetrate their interiors. Darkness is the incubator of fear. If we stay in the shade, we will always be vulnerable to its attack.

The first thing I did was visit a counselor who would help me untangle the spiderwebs I had spun in my head; that is to say, bring things to light. He helped me understand how the way I reacted to certain incidents in my life brought me to live in that depressive state all those years. He also helped me go through a process of pardoning some who had hurt me and asking forgiveness of some whom I had hurt (which is much more difficult). All of this brought the lie to light. The lie in my life was that "everyone" hated me. This is not true, yet I had begun to believe it. By understanding this, I began to realize that it was merely a product of my imagination. The light exposes all the lies and shows the truth. Another truth I had to confront was that my attitude and negativity had hurt many people, and I had to destroy the lie that I was "justified" in doing so because of x or y. I had to face the cruel and difficult reality that no one was responsible for my poor treatment of other people but me. As you can imagine, they were extremely difficult days for me before I finally began to see

a bit of light at the end of the tunnel. But once I began to see this light
. . . I cannot describe the freedom I began to experience! It's indescrib-
able! Light exposes fear. Fear cannot live in the light. We must walk
in the light, because with light, everything can be seen.

Some time ago, Miriam and I participated in a spiritual encounter with several people from the congregation we lead. One of
the activities involved walking to a remote site where we had a huge
bonfire. To get there we had to walk through a small forest and cross
over a bridge above a stream. We couldn't find a flashlight to illumi-
nate the way, but since I had passed by that way earlier in the day, I
thought I could find the path without much problem, so we decided
to do it without a flashlight. We could hear people speaking in the
distance; the faint light of the bonfire was visible, so I thought it
would be as easy as following the sound of the people and fixing our
eyes on the fire's light, but it was not.

It was around eleven at night and very dark. It was more than
dark. So much so that we couldn't see our hands in front of our faces.
My wife held on to me firmly by the arm because the darkness was so
profound that we couldn't even see our own thoughts, much less the
path. Fear began rising in her, until she declared that maybe we
would come across some lost alligator. I began to exaggerate, saying
that maybe there were tigers and lions ready to devour us. Miriam
kept insisting that we had found ourselves in an area of alligators and
that we should wait until we had a light to continue on our way to
the bonfire. She was so insistent that I put the doubt in my mind, too,
and I thought that any minute we would come across one of those
disagreeable reptiles. Thank the Lord, one of our associates finally

reached us with a lantern and from there on we could walk more safely without imagining alligators, waiting at the path's edge ready to snack on human flesh. Now we could see.

This is similar to what happens when we walk in spiritual darkness. Fear invades us and makes us think things that will probably never come to pass. Maybe we are imagining spiritual alligators crossing our path, ready to end our existence. This is why it's indispensable to walk in the light, so we can pass through life with a firm, sure step. The best way to get rid of fear is by destroying the darkness along our path. There is nothing better than simply to "Walk in the light as He is in the light" (1 John 1:7).

Life is an adventure in which each day gives rise to its own triumphs and victories, but also brings challenges and obstacles. If people ever told you they could give you the solution to your life and all your problems would disappear, they were telling you a fantasy. It simply doesn't work that way. If they ever told you that giving your life to the Lord would make all your problems go away and you'd never have another one, they were telling you a big lie. Nevertheless, we who have found Him on our life's path can declare words of hope for he who has none. The Lord is a great light that will help us walk with confidence. The obstacles, fears, doubts, and worries will be exposed by His great light, and will help us to live lives free from fear. The good news is also that we have a great ally to help us walk in confidence: Jesus Christ our Lord. It was He who said: "I am the light of the world, he who follows me will not walk in darkness, but will have the light of life" (John 8:12). When we walk in the light, there is no way to stumble because our step is strong and sure. "The Lord himself strengthens our steps when He is pleased with our way of life" (Psalms 37:23).

Obstacles in the Road

On beginning to change our life's path, we discover obstacles that we have to get rid of to advance. This truth made me carry out a study into which obstacles in life filled a person with fear. Upon investigation, I identified two main impediments. The first obstacle that brings fear and insecurity has to do with the practice of impure habits and ways of thinking that keep us in the darkness. The second obstacle has to do with memories of our pasts that bring insecurity to our lives. To start, I will list some of the habits that perhaps we consider normal in our lives but which I can assure you are not.

Fraud, Deceit, Fraudulent Business Deals

The practice of fraud and shady business is part of some people's daily lives. There is nothing worse than when a businessman panics while practicing dark business dealings. He never knows when he'll be discovered or what the consequences will be. His path will not be strong as long as he walks in this kind of darkness.

Some months ago, a man I knew came to speak with me because he recognized he had a big problem and needed help. For many years he had defrauded several people, many of them relatives. The amount of money he'd stolen exceeded tens of thousands of dollars. My friend found himself in a state of high tension because he knew his behavior was wrong. He lived with constant fear that one day he would be discovered, and it destroyed him to think of what would happen to himself and his family if his creditors took action against them. Not long before, he had completely turned his life over to the Lord and started coming weekly to our congregation in Houston. Thank the Lord, we were able to help him. He decided to bring everything to light, to face his situation, to look those friends and relatives he defrauded in the eye, and to start on the path toward restitution. I take my hat off to this great man.

This kind of act calls for a good deal of bravery. Walking in the light is not for the faint of heart. I knew for sure that once he began to journey on this path, God would restore my friend more than one could have imagined. There is no better way to live. Fear, doubt, and uncertainty go away. My friend has a smile on his face that only his wife and he can fully appreciate. After living in the shadow of his shady activity, they now live in the light. God rewards those who decide to leave the darkness and start walking in His light.

On the other hand, there was a man who involved us in a fraudulent scheme that he was carrying out. Everything seemed legit at the beginning, but it didn't take us long to realize that he had brought us a stream of lies, deceit, and theft. It had to do with cars that were repossessed by the bank. There was a period in Mexico, after the devaluation of the peso in '94, when the banks repossessed many cars because people had no means to pay for them. They had entire lots full of semi-new cars with literally tens of thousands of automobiles. Someone told us that a certain person was buying great numbers of these cars from the bank and was selling them at very reasonable prices. The bank gave them to him at a price well below their value, with the sole goal of getting rid of them. Our "friend" assured us that "since it was us" he wouldn't charge us big commissions, but pass the cars along to us at a price very near what they had cost him. The only thing he needed was a big deposit so he could buy the cars at the bank auction. That's where things began to take a wrong turn.

Many of our partners and friends took money out of their savings or sold some things to be able to pay the large down payments this person requested. When the first cars began to arrive, more people became convinced that this was legitimate and signed up to buy cars from him, too. They sent in their deposits and waited. Some of our friends did get their cars, but in very inferior condition: crashed, dented, not in the state that the person who sold them had promised they'd be in. Others simply never received theirs. More time passed, there were more calls, more uneasiness, more complaints, but nothing happened. It didn't take us long to realize that it was a scam that cost many dear people a lot of money—money they couldn't afford to lose. The last time I inquired, this individual was a fugitive from the law living in exile. He, unlike my friend in the congregation in Houston, chose to stay in his darkness. Instead of being brave, and bringing everything to light, he will live the rest of his life on the lam—fleeing from the law and from the people he defrauded, but worse than that, fleeing from the only thing that can bring him true personal freedom: the light. How horrible it is to live in darkness!

Sexual Immorality

Sexual immorality and promiscuity are other obstacles that block our path and subject us to fear. I knew a man who had three different families. He had become involved in a web so intricate that he lived looking for a way to hide one family from the others. What a miserable existence! To live in this kind of darkness is something I wouldn't wish on anyone. After this man died, it was not a pretty scene when two of his three wives came to the funeral. Both had always suspected that the other existed, but they had never been able to prove it until that afternoon, standing in front of his coffin. At the side of one woman was a boy of about fourteen who was identical to his father. At the side of the other was a boy of twelve years, also identical to the father. It looked like something out of a Cantinflas movie. Only it wasn't as funny because this was real life. How sad it was for me to see these two women fight like alley cats when they met in this place. Each one criticized the other for being there, and each was sure that she was the only one who had the "right" to act the role of the dead man's wife. The lack of commitment on this man's part, and his decision to always stay in the dark with respect to this great tragedy, brought disgrace and pain to all who sincerely loved him. The dark man will walk in his own darkness and will never be able to live in freedom. Instead, he'll be accompanied by shame and dishonor.

There is hope for all who want to be free. The Lord wants to give us freedom. It doesn't matter what shady activity we find ourselves in today. There can be freedom in our lives tomorrow. We don't have to keep walking in darkness. We can begin to walk the marvelous path of the light of God, Our Father.

Pornography

Today, millions of people indulge in pornography. They become introduced to this habit and to promiscuous thinking by believing that there is some pleasure in this illusion. But once they get involved, they can't find the doorway to freedom. The Internet, which is a marvelous tool with many positive uses, has become one of the most effective for turning victims into pornography addicts. In former times, people had to go to a store to buy pornographic magazines and videos. To some degree, this kept many from doing it for fear of being discovered in these infamous places. But today, computers give consumers of this sensual drug complete privacy by allowing them to see anything they want without leaving their houses. This habit has become the greatest income-producing business on the Internet.

It's sad to know the number of young people being trapped by this web of darkness and deceit. One out of every four young persons between the ages of ten and seventeen years is exposed to pornographic material, while one of every five receives an invitation to illicit sex by the same means. It has become a huge, unhealthy epidemic of immorality and promiscuity. Millions are getting caught up in activities that merely isolate, alienate, and leave them with emotional scars that, in many cases, last their lifetimes. All for not living in the light. What one must do in secret, doesn't have much legitimacy.

I recently read an article that says: "Pornography molds people's attitudes and behavior. This addiction can destroy trust and sincerity, indispensable qualities in a marriage. Since pornography is usually viewed in secret, whoever does so is obliged to lie to his or her partner (due to fear of being discovered). When the other finds out, he or she feels betrayed, and asks herself why her partner no longer finds her attractive. Pornography destroys the marital union" (author unknown).

If you, like millions of others, are fighting against pornography, don't be one of those who remains in the darkness. Remember that you can see everything better in the light. The fact of your having to remain in the darkness is invading you with a fear you don't have to bear. If we come out into the light, seeking the help necessary to beat our addiction, we will live in a new brightness that will surprise us. Get out of pornography! Come into the light!

The Occult, Esoteric Doctrines

Traveling the paths of the occult, the esoteric, black magic, tarot cards, etc., is a habitual practice for many people around the world. These days, there seems to be an outsize fascination with this theme. More movies, television programs, and novels are about dark themes. Some are dismissed as harmless entertainment that we needn't worry about. But I assure you that our enemy's plan is to turn it into something so common and everyday, so much a part of daily life, that its familiarity finally serves to enchain more people. Perhaps it's easy for some to think that involvement in these activities doesn't harm those who perform them, but let me tell you that he who answers your consultations is not your friend but your enemy, the devil. He wants to destroy your life and the lives of those around you. For that reason, he will enter your life in a way you least suspect to achieve his objective. Remember that with light everything can be seen more clearly. Any activity that requires darkness to perform must be suspicious, right?

I recall one time when Miriam and I visited a friend of the family's. She lived in a type of neighborhood where several apartments shared the same patio and from which you reached everyone's front door. When we arrived we saw an egg and some dove feathers in the window of one of our friend's neighbors. Truly, it surprised us because we had never seen anything like this. When we mentioned it, our friend explained that her neighbor was practicing some kind of esoteric activity and what we had seen in her window was the residue of some strange ceremony that she was always doing at night (darkness). Our friend continued telling us that her neighbor's family was always overwhelmed by tragedy: divorce, death, accidents, anguish, members of the family living in insane asylums, and so on. Personally, I haven't the faintest doubt of where the source of all that tragedy lies: the father of darkness. When we play his games, we get his results. If we play on his favorite team, we will accomplish all his goals, no doubt. If we play with fire, we get burned. What is there to do? Leave this darkness and walk in the light. It's that simple. Remember that, in the light, you can see everything better.

Wrath, Anger, and Mistreatment

Surely we all know people who behave one way in public and another way in private. In front of strangers they are the most marvelous people the world has ever seen, but when they are alone with their own families, they are angry, abusive, and insulting. Obviously, the person who hits his partner and his children has deep psycholog-ical, emotional, spiritual, and every other kind of problem, known and unknown. He needs professional help. Whoever mistreats his loved ones when the doors of his house are shut is a person who is living in darkness. Therefore, my advice would be: Come out of the darkness, abandon your wrath, anger, and ill treatment of others, and begin to walk in the light. Remember that you can see everything bet-ter in the light.

Lies

Many people struggle with lying and exaggeration. They exaggerate and blow everything out of proportion. A woman said to her son, "I've told you a million times not to exaggerate." A biblical proverb declares: "Better is the poor man than the liar" (Proverbs 19:22). It is very easy for some to lie, since they have a habit of building their life based on a lie. When you live with lies, you will always have to re-sort to a new one to hide the previous one. Lie after lie, all one's life lived like a big lie. What should we do? Come out into the light. We must live in the light of the truth of God's Word. We must leave the darkness of lies and begin walking in the light. God's truth dissipates all lies. The darkness of lies will be exposed by the light of truth. And remember that you can see everything better in the light.

Gossip

The gossip, the disseminator of discord, lives in fear. The Bible says: "A perverse man stirs up dissension, and a gossip separates close friends" (Proverbs 16:28). People who use their words to bring division and discord among friends, family, and loved ones are people whom God hates. The word *hates* seems pretty strong to me, yet God uses it to describe how He feels toward this type of person. Those who use these tactics are people living in darkness. What can be done? Go out into the light. Remember that you can see everything better in the light.

Uncontrollable Passions

Many things terrorize people who live enslaved to uncontrollable passions. For example, those who live tied to alcohol, drugs, gambling, and other vices cannot live in freedom. They live like slaves in the darkness of their addiction. The same happens to many who are food addicts. The city where we now live, Houston, Texas, has for many years earned the statistical ranking of being the fattest city in the United States. Many of the people in our city are food addicts.

> *Remember that man stays in his corner of darkness for fear that the light of truth will let him see things that would destroy his conjectures.*
>
> —J. J. Benitez

What must we do? Come out into the light. Remember that if we have an addiction of any type, we need to seek help and begin to walk in the light. Remember that you can see everything better in the light.

Don't Back Down

It's not easy to admit that our lives are full of particular situations like those I've listed here. But let me give you a word of hope, a map of the pathway to the long-awaited treasure, a way to freedom from fear.

Saint John the Apostle declared: "If we walk in the light, since God is in the light, we have fellowship with one another, and the blood of Jesus cleanses from us all sin" (1 John 1:7). He adds: "If we confess our sins, God is faithful and just and will pardon us and purify us from all unrighteousness" (1 John 1:9). To be able to walk in the light, all we need is to be born of the Lord. The Bible says that all who are born of God do not practice sin. Therefore, when we embrace God's nature, we begin to be like Him, we begin to feel an inexplicable repugnance for sin, and when we least expect it, we have left it to one side. Once we draw near to the Lord, He will help us live free of the darkness. He will guide us to the light. Remember that you can see everything better in the light.

To walk in the light is to walk in freedom, with the tranquillity of knowing that all our debts have been settled. There are no longer lies on our lips; we haven't defrauded anyone. We walk in the freedom with which Christ has made us free. However, if you believe that you need help and that you cannot leave the path of darkness by yourself, you should seek help. Do it! You will never regret having left the darkness. Remember you can see everything better in the light.

If we turn on a little light in our lives, fear will have nowhere to hide. It will have to leave. Turn on the light! With light, you can see everything better!

I want to end this chapter by presenting you with a challenge: Make a decision this very day. Decide to walk in the light and abandon the darkness.

The Lord says that if one is in Christ "He is a new creation; the old things pass away and everything is new" (2 Corinthians 5:17).

There is a new life waiting for you. Freedom for you. If you choose to walk in the light of the Word of God, you will have a new life. If suddenly that habit returns to knock on your door, you will tell it: "The old things have passed, in the Lord, everything in my life was made new." If fear comes to intimidate you and tell you that you are worthless, you are going to answer it: "I have chosen to follow the path that the light of the Word of God shows me, I will not turn back."

For Laughs

In the din of battle, the commander screams at his soldiers: "Go on! Who is in charge here, me or fear?"

A soldier who could no longer handle the challenge answers: "Fear!"

"What do you mean, fear?" his boss asks him.

"Sure, because you're very *commanding*, but fear is very *general*."

Reflection

1. Which obstacles, impure habits, and ways of thinking do I need to get rid of?

2. Are there negative things hidden in my life that I fear others will discover?

3. What areas need to be illuminated?

4. Would I be prepared to confess my mistakes, repent, and let myself be renewed?

5. Will I need professional help in addition to spiritual help?

Prayer

Heavenly Father, scrutinize my heart and my thoughts and take away all darkness and all the occult and negative that may reside therein. I want to walk in integrity, in Your truth and in Your light. Make me a resident of Your glory, and make of my heart Your dwelling. Strengthen my steps. I repent of my mistakes. Help me to walk in Your Word and in Your freedom. Thank You for being my light, for forgiving me, for helping me with each challenge, and for freeing me from all fear.

CHAPTER EIGHT

Turn Your Back on the Past

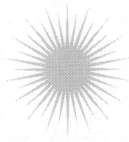

The inspirations of fear are fatal.
It is necessary to risk danger in order
to obtain victory.

—SIMÓN BOLÍVAR

We all make mistakes. It's part of the natural cycle of life. However, a mistake that is even greater than making a mistake is to keep living the mistake. Many people become so choked by a mistake that it paralyzes them in other areas of their lives. They stop feeling happy, being creative, imagining that good things even exist for them. The mistake holds them back to such a degree that it seems as if they build a shrine to it, light candles, place floral offerings in front of it, and sing it songs, celebrating it, instead of correcting it by burying it once and for all. It's time to turn our backs on the past, call the mistake history, and begin to prepare ourselves for a great future. We can never conquer what is in the past. We can only conquer what's in our future. Make a decision! Turn your back on the past.

After going to an advisor who helped me untangle the spiderwebs in my head, I very clearly recall a session during which he said to me, "Marcos, you simply must let go of the past and look toward the future." He said it in relation to a profound preoccupation I had with some people whom my actions had hurt deeply, a situation there was no way to correct. For years I had been lugging around these bundles of regret, pain, and guilt, believing that carrying these emotions would be adequate punishment to repay the pain I had caused. Thank the Lord, after many sessions of advice and prayer, I could begin to leave some of these burdens in the hands of God, understanding that the only one who could fix things was Him, not me. It didn't help me to carry around this emotional load. He had already carried all our guilt, pain, mistakes, and defects when He died for us on Calvary. I had to accept, on faith, my freedom and begin to live in a different way. I promise you that it was neither immediate nor easy. To the contrary, it is a process I am still involved in. There are times when I feel tempted to go back to the wastebasket and start searching for this burden to carry again. It doesn't take me long to find it, because I carried it for such a long time. I know it well. However, it does nothing but make me feel bad, guilty, and anxious. Sometimes we are slow to learn. I am still learning to leave this burden behind. There's no point in taking it up again. The same is true for you. Don't go back to the past in search of your mistakes. Join with me in the effort to leave the past behind. Make a firm, sure decision, to turn your back on the past.

The only things from the past that we need to keep carrying with us are the good lessons that we've learned, the rich memories that have made us the people we are today. I recall, for example, the time my dad rescued me from the Pacific Ocean, and my heart fills with happiness and joy at having a father like him. The fact that he isn't my biological father gives the story an even richer dimension: a stepfather who "adopted" me with such dedication and so much love that he was ready to lose his life saving me. How incredible! I will never turn my back on that enormous incident in my life. It marked me forever. It made me know, with absolute certainty, that the Lord has His hand on my life. This type of memory should be the only kind we carry with us for the rest of our lives. We should remember mistakes, pain, and the sorrows of the past only to learn how to never repeat them again; but carrying around guilt, regret, and bitterness will only submerge us in a sticky sentimental mire that will impede us from living anxiety-free lives.

The day I found myself seated at the command of a small plane with an examiner in the position of copilot, I was more nervous than usual. After five months of instruction, I'd flown a certain number of hours solo and with an instructor, and had completed many maneuvers to demonstrate my prowess as an airplane pilot. Now my teacher required me to pass the flight exam if I wanted to become licensed. My pilot friends tell me it is a day on which they all felt more nervous than usual. They also said that nearly all of them committed some kind of error because of the challenge of having that examiner seated by their side, carefully analyzing every action they made. My case was no exception. I was very nervous and apprehensive.

The flight went well at first. We took off smoothly and began traveling in the direction the examiner had assigned me the day before. He had asked that we use a flying technique that included looking for specific reference points on a map, locating them on the ground as we passed them, measuring the time between both points to calculate certain critical information such as velocity, fuel consumption, and so on. It is a system that pilots used before the advent of modern, sophisticated navigational systems. In other words, it is a truly antiquated system, but one which every pilot should know how to use in case there is an emergency and his electronic equipment stops working. In my five months of studying, I had mastered this navigational system. With my own instructor, I had never made a mistake. I had always found my points of reference, my calculations had always been correct; in short, I never thought I'd make a mistake. That is, until the day of the most important flight of my fledgling career as an airplane pilot.

I got lost! Plain and simple. I didn't have the slightest idea where we were. I couldn't find my second reference point on my flight plan. I'd fixed my eyes on something on the horizon that looked like my reference point, but the closer we got to it, the more I realized that it wasn't the reference point I had chosen. I'd been looking at the wrong thing. I quickly began looking all around me to see if by chance I could find the correct point. No way! The more I searched, the more desperate I grew. And, worse, while I was moving my head around looking for the reference point, our flight was suffering severely. The direction of the plane began to resemble an "S" lying down in the air, as I maneuvered the plane from side to side, trying desperately to find my reference point. During all this time, the instructor remained totally silent, waiting patiently for me to do something to rescue the situation. When he finally broke his silence, it was to get my attention and redirect my efforts.

"We're lost," the instructor said. "We've been lost a good while. You haven't shown me your second point of reference and you're still looking for it. We passed it more than five minutes ago. I saw it. Now you are turning circles in the air and you have us traveling all over the airspace, trying to find your second reference point that you passed way back. I want you to look at the map, look in front of you, and tell me a point on the ground that you can identify on the map." He asked me to do this three or four times until he was convinced that I could read maps. After that, we switched to another activity and continued the flight test, but I was doubting that I'd passed simply because a pilot who gets lost can't be a very good pilot.

When we concluded the flight, the instructor took a long time giving me a summary of his analysis. He told me that, in his opinion, I was a good pilot. He congratulated me a good deal for certain maneuvers that I had performed nearly perfectly. He also told me that my landings were the best he'd ever seen, a comment that was deeply gratifying, because I'd practiced my landings for so many hours, indeed, whole days. Then he began to analyze the subject of our getting lost. In short, he told me that the problem is that when I made the mistake, I didn't leave it in the past but carried it along with me for the rest of the flight. He told me that when one makes this type of mistake, the first thing you have to do is react quickly, analyze the situation, and go on piloting the plane. In this way, you maintain total control of the situation instead of letting the situation control you. In other words, by searching for my second point of reference, I had essentially stopped flying the plane competently. We were making circles in the air, going up and down in altitude—a fairly dangerous thing. By not leaving my mistake behind, I put the future of the flight in jeopardy. When my instructor said these words, without his knowing it, he was speaking to a much deeper part of my character, to who I am. I am very prone to not moving forward until I correct the error at hand. It's part of my nature. I've been this way most of my life. The problem with being like this lies not in the part of me wanting to fix the mistakes, but in taking the mistakes with me into the future, putting everything at risk and in danger. If only I were a person who could leave things in the past, my future would be much more secure. That day, my flight examiner helped me discover an aspect of my personality that, to this day, has helped me leave the past alone. It's true, I passed the flight exam, they gave me my pilot's license, I have more than two thousand hours of flight in my logbook, and I've never gotten lost again. I learned something that day.

The American Psychological Association's *Diagnostic and Statistical Manual of Mental Disorders* considers phobia an extreme fear of a specific object or situation. A phobia sufferer can have a panic attack if faced with the object or situation, and it is estimated to affect 10 percent of the population at some time in their lives. According to what has been registered, there are 6,596 phobias to date. Studies show that past traumatic situations predispose people to phobias. For example, people who have been in a car accident are more likely to panic while driving, or if parents suffer from a particular phobia, it is more likely that their children will suffer from it, too, because children copy their parents' behavior. Traumas from the past contribute greatly to the fears of today. For this reason, it is so important to battle these traumas.

In the previous chapter I mentioned how, upon researching fears, I identified two impediments or obstacles that slow our paths in life. The first was impure habits and practices or dishonest customs, which we have already examined. The second obstacle in the lives of people who are overwhelmed by fear is the influence of negative personal experiences in their pasts. I believe that this is one of the resources that our enemies use most to keep us under the control of fear. Over the course of our lives, we have all accumulated disagreeable memories, difficult personal experiences, some more negative than others, but we all have to look at our pasts to face those aspects of it that are slowing down our present. For many people, their pasts are no more than a series of lies that they must destroy to move forward. Some, for example, have taken responsibility for horrible past experiences that have nothing to do with them.

I know women who were raped as girls and, for their whole lives, have carried a mistaken guilt, thinking that they somehow were responsible. This prevents them from having good relationships in their adult lives and keeps them from living fear-free lives. It is time to destroy the lies about your past that you may have believed until now. Satan, the enemy of our souls, has been using these memories to keep us imprisoned, terrorized, and paralyzed, but I promise we will get out of this jail of the past and we will walk victoriously to the land of our dreams and our destiny in the Lord.

Our memory is like a computer's hard drive. I've sometimes joked that the hard drive of some is harder than that of others. The truth is, we all have recorded memories. Some have more memories than others, but everyone has the opportunity to enter one's hard drive and modify that archive that affects the workings of the computer's other activities. At times, when viruses get in, they can affect the good behavior of the entire computer. On these occasions, computer experts know how to get inside, correct the affected archives, take out what must be removed, and repair what must be repaired. It's the same thing that many of us need to do. There are certain archives in the hard drives of our memory that are damaged, and we need help from one who knows about this sort of thing (the maker of the hard drive, God) to enter us and help us repair those problems. Take out what needs to come out, reinstall what needs to be reinstalled, and reformat whatever needs to be reformatted. For this to happen, the fragments of our memories that have been damaged by bad experiences need to be repaired. Here are some of the possible repairs.

Forgiveness

We have in our hands the power to decide which thoughts we will permit to govern us. One of the most effective weapons our enemy uses to frighten us is our own memory. For example, if in the past someone hurt us and that memory was recorded on our heart, and we think about it every day, then we need to pardon that person and let go of those thoughts that belong in the past. Don't do like I did on the day of my examination and keep going back searching for the mistake. No. We must forgive, leave that memory in the past, and keep going forward. Our future is brilliant. That pain taught us something, but we must continue to fly the airplane of our lives.

Resentment hurts the vessel in which it is stored more than the object on which it is poured.

(Anonymous)

Our Lord Jesus taught about the importance of forgiveness when He said: "If you don't forgive men their offenses, neither will our Father forgive us our offenses" (Matthew 6:15). Many ask why their relationship with God seems to be obstructed or arrested. It might be due to a lack of forgiveness in their lives. The lesson is clear: If we don't forgive ourselves, neither will we be forgiven. It's as simple as that. We need to know that a lack of forgiveness is an enormous obstacle to our spiritual life. It's an enormous obstacle to getting to know the Lord better. We can't allow ourselves to live imprisoned. It's time to leave the past behind and advance toward the objective of our life, our promised land, our destiny in the Lord.

A well-known proverb says: "A man's good sense detains his rage, and it is to his glory to overlook an offense" (Proverbs 19:11). When someone offends us without our responding, that person thinks he got away with it; what he doesn't know is that offending us gives us a great opportunity to be more decent and honorable. Overlooking an offense simply means we don't give it undue importance. We are simply going to overlook it. If we let it settle in our hearts, we will have terrible problems. Nothing good comes from letting the offense become our roommate. If we let it into our house, we'll have to host it for many years, and I assure you it is a disorderly, dirty, undisciplined guest that we don't want. The best thing is to help it pack its suitcases and personally escort it to the bus station. Simply overlook the offense and never let it come to stay in your house.

Nailed to the cross, after having been the object of mass ridicule, having been beaten, falsely accused, made fun of in public, humiliated in front of his friends, followers, and family, our Lord Jesus proclaimed loudly: "Forgive them, Father, they know not what they do" (Luke 23:34). If we all could have that kind of love, the world would be a much more beautiful place. Jesus did not enumerate the sins of all those present, throwing them in their faces, but simply with a sentence, with His huge heart, He forgave everyone. You say: "Well, I am not Jesus, I don't have these same powers." But you can have them. We can all have them. If we invite Him to become part of our

daily lives, we can have this forgiving nature. Remember that each
time after the first time you forgive, that it becomes easier.

RESTITUTION

Many times when we think of memories, we always think of those
who hurt us. However, it's not always the case that others are the
ones who hurt us; rather, it's possible that we have hurt others. This
bad recollection brings guilt to our memory and is another weapon
that our enemy uses to make us live in fear and darkness. That
was my case. I couldn't stand the pain that came with the memory
of the wounds I had caused other people, and it was dramatically affecting my state of mind. This reality becomes more palpable for
people who have a great sensitivity toward others and don't want
to hurt them. When we know we have caused someone pain, or
treated that person badly, our lives simply become embittered. I know
others, however, who seem to have a protective coating around
their feelings. Nothing hurts them. They don't care what people
think of them. They can say what they want and not be affected.
It's very hard for me to understand this because I am exactly the opposite. I am too sensitive, and am very affected by what others think
or say about me. When I discovered that a big part of my anxiety had
to do with the pain I stored in my heart because of the grief I had
caused others, that immensely helped me to refocus my mind toward
correcting the situation. Here is where the part about restitution
comes in. In some cases, we can make restitution. In others, it's too late

and we just have to keep moving forward and let the Lord be our defense and our justice.

Restitution means making the effort, as much as possible, to repair the damage we have done to another person. It is one of the solutions the Lord gives us to help free us from our pasts. The action of restitution brings happiness. One of the best-known examples is one we find in the New Testament upon reading about the life of a wealthy tax collector named Zacchaeus.

Zacchaeus's life was one of endless plundering. He was a man of shady business dealings and usually robbed people through his efforts. However, Jesus saw him perched on this sycamore tree and told him He wanted to visit him in his house. We can imagine that everybody was surprised, for this man was fairly well known in the land. Everyone had been ripped off by him. We can imagine that many of them asked each other, "How is it possible that Jesus will go eat with Zacchaeus in his house? Doesn't Jesus know who this guy is? I can't believe it." In studying Jesus' life, I am fascinated to know that He never turns his back on anyone. He visited everyone, fellowshipped with everyone, not caring what others thought. He turned his back on no one.

Jesus' visit to his home moved Zacchaeus profoundly. We don't know the details of their conversation, nor what happened that night in that dining room. What we do know is that Zacchaeus was so moved by the presence of Jesus that his life was forever changed. That is the effect that Jesus has on everyone's life. At one point that night, that man stood up before everyone and confessed his sins. The interesting thing about this public confession was not that Zacchaeus exposed his sins, because everyone was familiar with this man's life. The great miracle was what he added: "Here, Lord, I give half of my possessions to the poor; and if I have defrauded anyone, I will repay them in quadruplicate" (Luke 19:8). Can you imagine the amount of money Zacchaeus had, to be able to repay each one of the victims four times more than what he had stolen from them? Can you imagine the euphoria that reigned in that dining room when he gave the news to his guests? Can you imagine what the headlines of the newspapers would have been the next day, if there had been any? Can you imagine the conversations at the dinner tables of each family in that city? Jesus had passed through Zacchaeus's home and his life would never be the same. The visit to his house not only affected Zacchaeus but each person he had cheated and every poor person in the city. What Zacchaeus did, by returning four times more than what he'd stolen, is called "restitution." The power of restitution touches many lives. In some cases, we need to look for the people we have injured and find a way of making restitution. It will bring health to our hearts and to theirs.

My father, of whom I often speak with such pride, told us that in his childhood he had been a cashier in an ice cream shop. He was seventeen years old, and pinball machines were in vogue at that time. Since he was in charge of the cash register, he had access to the money they got from the sale of the ice cream cones. When no one was looking, he took twenty-five-cent coins to play the pinball machines. He had a good time and a while passed without him thinking he was hurting anyone, despite knowing that taking this money was wrong. More than five years would go by before he gave his life to Jesus in a personal and practical manner. As he came to know more about God and His principles, something from his past began to bother him: the twenty-five-cent coins he had taken for pinball. It bothered him so much that he calculated the amount he'd taken, wrote a letter to the owner of the store, and sent him a check for the amount he'd stolen. In the letter he explained to the owner that he had recently come to know the truth of God through Jesus Christ and this new life made him regret what he had done in the past, and he asked for forgiveness. He asked that the man accept the check as restitution for what he'd been robbed of. My dad said the owner wrote him back, thanking him profoundly for his honesty and for the check. He encouraged him to keep traveling in this new life he had found with God. My father has recently passed, but he continued walking this path with God until the end of his life. He was an admirable man. This experience of restitution is one of the reasons I personally believe my father was honored by the Lord his whole life. It is a great example to follow. When the Lord sees in our hearts this decision to make restitution for the damages we have caused others, I can imagine He has a party in heaven. I imagine the angels summoning a mariachi band, starting to dance, and you and I starting to live a new kind of victory. Restitution is one of the keys that opens the prison of fear and lets us get out *free*.

Memories That Tie Us Down

As I did for years, many of us live with memories that stop us, bind us, and don't permit us to leave the jail of fear. Some simply because forgiveness is difficult for them. Others because they have been hurt so deeply, they can't let go of the pain. They somehow justify themselves by thinking that their disagreeable memories simply guarantee them the right to hold on to their pain and suffering. Others don't let go of disagreeable memories simply for reasons of hatred, bitterness, and vengeance. They want to retain the memory until the perfect moment when, given the right circumstances, they can take revenge on the persons who hurt them.

I don't understand their reasons for keeping the memories alive and not letting go of the past. Come what may, everyone loses when they do not walk the path of forgiveness, restitution, and restoration. When we succeed in having the spirit of Christ, who forgave even as He was hanging on the cross, we all win. If we cling to these memories, we will be bound to them for the rest of our lives. Let go of them and let yourself live in the freedom that comes from leaving the past behind so that you can realize the brilliance of your future. Turn your back on the past.

THREATS

A little while ago a family came to tell me the following: "Marcos, we are frightened because we've received death threats." Because of a situation in their workplace, someone had threatened them. These people had been living with the fear of this threat, which is a fear that incarcerates many people. Some folks threaten others by saying, "I'm going to take you to court." Unfortunately, we live in the most litigious era in history. Those who receive these kinds of threats carry that burden and live with worry, thinking, They'll probably throw me in jail, or maybe they'll kill me. What will become of me?

The Bible says that the accuser is called the devil, and he uses his voice only to accuse and point a finger. You must go forth into the light and let the Word of God guide you in all your dealings. You need to sing the Word of God, you need to declare the Word of God, you need to fill your surroundings with the Word of God. Begin to recite Bible verses like the one that says: "No weapons used against you will prosper, and you will condemn every tongue that is lifted against you in judgment" (Isaiah 54:17). The Word of God has the power to break the threat and bring to naught the lies Satan would love for us to embrace.

REJECTION

Our enemy uses memories of rejection against a great many people. If someone rejects us, we feel humiliated. All of us have felt rejection at some time in our lives. In one of the earlier chapters, I wrote about my problem when I was a small boy, my tremendous ability for wetting the bed every night. Everyone made fun of me, especially when I began to grow up and turn twelve, thirteen, fourteen years of age, and I still wet the bed. Many years later, the Lord helped me achieve victory over this teasing that I experienced as rejection, and which brought many disagreeable emotional consequences to my life. Thank God that as of today I have remained free of that rejection and also, thank the Lord, I no longer wet the bed.

The Bible says: "The Lord chooses the lowly things and the despised things—and the things that are not—to nullify the things that are" (1 Corinthians 1:28). God selects the vile and the unappreciated to become His vessels. If someone rejects another, he or she did that person a big favor, because the rejected one becomes a candidate for being used for the glory of God. So enjoy yourself and be happy. If you haven't been rejected yet, don't worry, your turn will come.

In Latin America and in the world, we have a tremendous abandonment problem. Many fathers abandon their families to start new ones; husbands abandon their wives for other women. It is an epidemic on our continent that brings many negative consequences to the families that experience it. I once spoke with a young man whose father had left him when he was a baby. He never knew him and would not see him again until he was seventeen years old. Sadly, this is the story of many young people. Upon reconnecting with his father, this young man had many questions for him: "Why did you leave us? Why did you go?" Because these memories mark many of our infancies and childhoods, we live submerged in fear, in anguish, in the darkness of not knowing why things happened. In many cases, children take the blame for the abandonment and suffer disastrous psychological effects. From there, many let the bitterness and rancor into their lives that this tenacious resentment represents. Nothing good can come of this. We have to leave the past behind, conquer our future, and have the knowledge that the Lord has great things waiting for us tomorrow. Let go of those memories. Turn your back on the past.

What to Do?

Resentment, bitterness, and hatred are very clear foundations that, with time, can provoke important illnesses, many of them terminal. Resentment, bitterness, and hatred serve no good purpose. Leave them in the past and walk toward your future. In his book to the Romans, Saint Paul the Apostle says: "Don't avenge yourselves, my beloved ones, rather leave room for the wrath of God; because it is written: Vengeance is mine, I will repay, says the Lord" (Romans 12:19). Remember that God can handle your enemies better than you can. Let the vengeance of God take place. We cannot do justice like the Lord can. It's time to leave some things in God's capable hands and simply turn our backs on those painful memories that we cannot change. It is time to let God take charge of us. Let Him heal our wounds, let Him make justice, let Him bring us to a better tomorrow. Turn your back on the past. Your future is much better.

Faced with an injustice or adversity, the first emotion to arise is the desire for revenge. But if we practice vengeance we are not letting the Lord take charge of things. Our mentality must be that: "God can handle these things much better than I ever could." Hatred signifies antipathy and aversion. Many people express hatred hidden behind their declarations: "I hope things go badly for him and that he can never get ahead." It serves no purpose to have this bitterness and rancor inside us, and at the same time I assure you it doesn't help the person you feel this rancor against. He probably doesn't even know you're mad at him. Let it go! Be free to live in victory, without fear.

The prophet Isaiah said: "Forget about former things, neither bring to memory the past" (Isaiah 43:18). Let's no longer remember the memories of the past; let's forget those offenses, the abandonment, rejection, or whatever else we have suffered. Let us abandon the past and embrace the new that God has in store for us.

For Laughs

The patient arrives to tell the psychiatrist his problem.

"Doctor, I have a problem: every time I go to lie down, I think there's someone under the bed. To combat this, I lie down under the bed and then I think there's someone above me. You have to help me or I'm going to go crazy!"

The specialist was thoughtful, and then he answered, "Put yourself in my hands for twelve months. Come three times a week to see me and I will cure you of your fears."

"How much do you charge per session?" the guy asked him warily.

"Five hundred dollars a visit."

"Okay, doctor. I'll think about it and I'll let you know."

Six months later the psychiatrist ran into this individual in the street and asked, "Why didn't you come back to see me?"

"For five hundred dollars a visit? My buddy cured me for the price of just one dinner."

"Oh, yes? How did he do it?" the doctor asked skeptically.

"He told me to cut all four legs off the bed."

For Laughs

A woman runs into her neighbor in the street and says; "Hey, excuse me, but you owe me ten dollars."

Her neighbor answers: "I excuse you, I excuse you."

Reflection

Meditate on your memories and write down the names of all those who directly or indirectly injured or hurt you. Then make a list of those persons whom you have injured and to whom you'd like to make some kind of restitution.

After facing the truth of your annotations, make some decisions, resolve these memories in your mind to be able to move on. Nothing we retain from the past helps us face the future.

Ask God to help you not remain in this place, but move forward to resolve the pain you have suffered.

1. Am I still tied to my past?

2. What are the disagreeable memories from my past that still threaten me and that I need to stop remembering?

3. Do I have bitterness, guilt, resentment, or a lack of forgiveness in my heart?

4. Whom do I need to forgive and whom must I ask to forgive me?

5. For which things should I repent and be renewed?

6. What should I leave in God's hands for Him to do justice?

Prayer

Good and compassionate Father, I recognize that I have made mistakes in the past and that I have memories that do not benefit me. I repent for all the harm I've caused other people and I forgive those who have done me harm. I ask that you take all guilt, resentment, hatred, bitterness, feelings of rejection, and lack of forgiveness from my life and set me free. Thank You for being my light and my liberation, for forgiving me, restoring me, and erasing my past. Thank You for making everything new.

CHAPTER NINE

Face Tomorrow

Don't be afraid of tomorrow.
God is already there.

—John Mason

The first time I visited Disneyland, I was five years old. My entire family had made the trip to visit my grandparents, who lived in a nearby city. Because of my young age, I don't recall many details of that trip, but I have a very clear memory of the night before we went to visit that place so loved by children around the world. I could hardly sleep, I was so excited. I had seen photos and television programs about it, but I was sure nothing could compare with the reality of visiting it. At school, I had some friends who had been there and returned telling marvelous, fantastic stories about everything they did. I almost couldn't contain my desire to go. As I lay awake, I asked myself a thousand questions: "Will I get to meet Mickey? What will Cinderella's Castle be like? Will Donald, Pluto, and all the rest be there?" I would have given anything to wake up and be there already. What expectations. What wishes for morning to arrive. What enthusiasm when I awoke.

This is how we can live if we turn our backs on the past, overcome our fear, let light into our lives, and live with perfect love, forgiveness, restitution, and restoration. What an exciting way to live! You can await the future with great enthusiasm, faith, and hope, knowing that the best is yet to come. If we awaken every day with the same kind of enthusiasm that I had upon waking up that morning to visit Disneyland, every day would be different for us. We wouldn't see life as a monotonous routine, but with expectation and admiration, wanting to know what good things will happen to us. If we see every day as a trip to our favorite place, our daily activities will turn into daily adventures. Fear lives in pessimism and negativity because of their dark, gloomy activities. If we live with optimism and expectation, life will smile on us more. We'll know better how to take advantage of opportunities. We'll understand how to get the best out of every day, moment, and thing to come. Face tomorrow with enthusiasm!

When the United States embarked upon its space program in 1958, seven men were chosen to become the first astronauts. Imagine the excitement of Scott Carpenter, Gordon Cooper, John Glenn, Gus Grissom, Walter Schirra, Alan Shepard, and Deke Slayton. They had been chosen to go where no one had gone before. Yet as astronauts, they knew that they would have to face danger, challenges, and unforeseen tests. Every one of them knew that the excitement of being chosen presented them with the challenge of an unknown future. Nevertheless, they had personally determined that the risk was worth it for the future that they would acquire for the world. They weighed the fear of the unknown against the triumph of tomorrow and decided that the triumph won. In spite of the fact that only one of the original seven—Alan Shepard—made it to the moon, they were willing to run the risk so that one day *someone* would reach it. In fact, some astronauts gave their lives to the cause by dying in a horrible accident that set back the entire program. But if you could ask them about their participation in the project, I am sure that, because of the inherent optimism each one of them possessed, they would tell us that giving their lives would have been an acceptable risk. They had already calculated that risk and it didn't stop them. How admirable! This is why they are heroes.

One of the best ways we can destroy fear is by looking toward the future. The words of the prophet Jeremiah declare a secret that should accompany us every day of our lives: " 'Because I know the thoughts I have about you,' says The Lord, 'the plans to prosper you and not to harm you, plans to give you hope and a future' " (Jeremiah 29:11). To begin with, it thrills me to know that the Lord thinks about me. In the second place, to know that His thoughts are good, benevolent, full of peace. God is not thinking of how to destroy me or punish me for what I've done poorly. He knows I am mortal and I, like everyone, make mistakes. God is not thinking of how to execute a judgment against me for some foolishness I have committed. In fact, one of the reasons Jesus Christ died on Calvary for every one of us was to satisfy the need for judgment. The Lord poured out His judgment against Jesus by His being nailed to the cross. God now has peaceful thoughts toward us, because He views us through His son, Jesus. The thoughts of the Lord for us are so good that we can aspire to be successful in what we do, because He will help us. In fact, God created us to triumph. I don't think there is a single person about whom God thought, "Okay, I'm going to make this one to fail in life." Never! It's impossible! The Lord made us to be triumphant, and so great is His wish that we triumph that He thinks about us. He thinks about what He can do to give us the end we desire. He thinks about giving us a future full of hope. The Lord is a God of hope, not of yesterday. God is a God who wants us to see the next day. God is in our tomorrow. If we succeed in seeing ourselves in tomorrow, He will be waiting for us there. Stop looking at your yesterday. By doing so, you are blind to tomorrow. We must learn to think how God thinks: thoughts of peace and hope.

The future God planned for our lives is full of hope, blessings, happiness, and abundance. If we always think about the mistakes we made yesterday, or if we believe that we will always live as slaves, then we are giving in to a spirit of fear that we must defeat. Let's beat it once and for all to go ahead with our futures. We've wasted too much time on yesterday. Now is the time to go forward, to look toward tomorrow. The view is beautiful. Come see it with me.

BLIND TO THE PAST

The life of Saul of Tarsus was an absolute disaster. He had a terrible past that haunted him endlessly. The Bible describes him as breathing murderous threats (Acts 9:1) against those who believed in Christ. His worst enemies were those who did not believe the same way he did, and he never left them in peace. He pursued them, but not to inquire or see what their opinions were, or to study their habits and understand why they were so devoted to this Jesus. He followed them merely with a zeal to kill them. You read it right. He killed them. He gathered the necessary permits from the religious leaders to go into a city and ask who the followers of Jesus were, and with his legal permits in hand, he took them to the outskirts of the city and had them stoned to death. His hatred of Christians was so deep and profound that what he did didn't affect him in the least. He did the same thing, place after place, city after city. He was well known throughout the region. Everyone knew who Saul of Tarsus was, and when they found out that he'd entered a city, I can imagine the chaos and fear it provoked.

But one fine day, on the way to the city of Damascus, Saul of Tarsus had an encounter with Jesus that would change his life forever. It was one of those spectacular encounters, like in a movie. A great light shone from the heavens, knocking him off his horse; he fell to the ground, blind, crawling around, trying to find out where he was. The great and terrible Saul of Tarsus reduced in an instant to a blind man, crawling on the ground without knowing where he was nor what had happened. The Lord certainly has ways of getting one's attention.

Lying on the ground, he heard a powerful voice from the heavens ask him why he was persecuting him. Upon hearing that, Saul asked, "Who are you, sir?" The answer came: "I am Jesus, the one you are persecuting." Saul of Tarsus's answer helps us understand why he was the great man that he was. He was smart. It didn't take him long to understand or figure things out. He quickly responded: "What do you want me to do?" When the Lord told him what to do that afternoon, Saul's life changed entirely and would never be the same again (Acts 9:3–7).

After that encounter with Jesus, Saul remained blind for three days. He entered the city of Damascus guided by friends who brought him to the path that led to the house of the person who would help him move forward, a man called Ananias. The fact that he remained blind is interesting, because many times, to look toward our tomorrows we need to remain blind to our yesterdays. Looking at our past keeps us from seeing our future. Saul had to remain blind so that on awakening to his new reality, he had a new perspective, a new way of seeing things. Three days later, after Ananias prayed for the blindness of Saul of Tarsus, he was given sight and began to walk in his new life. Only this time he would live in a very different way from how he had been living—a new course, new directions, new instructions, a new destiny. From having been Saul of Tarsus, terrible and feared for killing Christians, he would go on to become one of the greatest Christian theologians in history. He would become the most prolific writer of the New Testament, Paul the Apostle.

Yet even after his transformation, people doubted him because they feared his infamous reputation. There is a well-known saying in Latin America: "Make yourself famous and then take it easy." Saul of Tarsus was famous. Everyone knew he was the "Christian killer" and now he went all over saying that an encounter with Jesus had changed his life. Many years would pass before people freed him from his past. Time proved that Saul had, in effect, had a new beginning. In a letter he wrote to the church he founded in Rome, Paul would say: "Do not conform to this century but be transformed by the renovation of your mind, so that you will be able to test and approve what God's will is—His good, pleasing and perfect will" (Romans 12:2). To be able to face tomorrow, we need to ask God to help us change our way of thinking. The Lord does not want us to see things like we have always seen them, but to see them as He sees them. God wants to give us a new way of seeing.

Mobilized for What Lies Ahead

After Saul regained sight and his life changed, the text says: "In the synagogues he immediately preached that Christ was the Son of God" (Acts 9:20). The blow Saul of Tarsus had received that afternoon on the way to Damascus mobilized him immediately toward his new future. He didn't stay waiting to see what was going to happen in his life or when his new job would begin. Rather, he immediately got up and began to preach. Today there are those of us who have an encounter with Jesus and receive a new perspective on life, but instead of taking immediate action, as Saul did, we remain still, complacent, and quiet. Some of us because of indecision, others out of fear, and still others out of ignorance. Whichever the case may be, my advice is that we take the example of this extraordinary man and act as quickly as possible. Saul of Tarsus's first impulse was to go out and conquer his future and express what he felt inside. "But Saul made an even greater effort, and perplexed the Jews who gossiped in Damascus demonstrating that Jesus was Christ" (Acts 9:22).

It surprised me to read later that the story tells that some people wanted to kill Saul of Tarsus, but then he "Spoke daringly in the name of the Lord, and argued with the Greeks, but they endeavored to kill him" (Acts 9:29). Let me say something from my own experience: It doesn't matter what you want to be, how great or small your vision, I can guarantee you that as soon as you begin to act, there will always be people who want to destroy you. Jesus Christ Himself promised us so, saying: "I have told you these things so you have peace in me. In the world you will have affliction, but trust me, I have conquered the world" (John 16:33). Generally, those who wish to kill us are the ones who are doing nothing. That's why they have the time to plan the death of someone who is acting. But don't worry about those who want to kill you, just keep moving. That is what impressed me when I read the story of Saul of Tarsus—he kept on going, he kept on moving. True success comes with persistence, perseverance. Put one foot in front of the other and don't let anyone stop you. Saul of Tarsus, later Paul the Apostle, was one of the most extraordinary men in history. He went from a terrible past to great historical prominence. In the same way, the Lord wants to take you and me from our terrible pasts and carry us to a very high place. If we accept the challenge, we can write the new story of our lives, our families, and our countries. We could also help others become champions.

Advice for a Safe Journey

Put Your Past in Order

Few things in the past are irreparable but this should not stop you. We should leave them behind, in the past and to oblivion, and advance toward what lies ahead. Remember what the Word of God promises: "So that someone is in Christ, he is a new being; the old shall pass; all I have here is new" (2 Corinthians 5:17). The Lord takes our pasts and makes everything new in our lives.

I remember the story a little old preacher told us when I was still a child. He said that when the Lord removed our sins, He took them to a special place called the Sea of Oblivion. We were told it was a very deep sea that no one could enter, where our sins remained at the bottom and it was impossible to retrieve them. God put a big sign on the sea, saying NO FISHING in case someone tried to retrieve our mistakes and sins and remind us of them. God hid our past in such a way that He wouldn't even let anyone fish in the Sea of Oblivion. I invite you not to fish in that sea, either. It serves no purpose. Leave them where they are, in oblivion, hidden by the powerful grace of God, purchased by Jesus' perfect sacrifice.

Dream

I have only three words of advice to say about dreaming and they are:

1. Dream!

2. Dream!

3. Dream!

Dream when you are asleep. Dream when you are awake. Dream while you are seated. Dream while you are eating. Dream and dream, and when you've finished dreaming, dream some more. It's difficult for me to understand why so many people refuse to dream. It costs nothing, it's highly entertaining, and what's more, it's the cradle of many good ideas that can give rise to great realities. When we think about facing tomorrow, it's indispensable that we dream. There is no future if we do not dream. Your dreams can be the strongest and most effective antidote to your fears. I read the saying that goes: "The hero and the coward feel exactly the same way in regard to fear; the only difference is that the hero confronts his fears and turns them into fire." Do not run away; confront your fears and begin to dream. See yourself with a trophy in hand, with the winner's check in your bank account. Begin to walk like a champion, think like a champion, see yourself as a champion, and dream like a champion. Adopt the winner's attitudes and begin to see yourself as such. If you don't see yourself winning, triumphing, arising, advancing, conquering, seizing, planting the seeds and reaping their harvest, then it will never become a reality in your life. You have to see it in your heart before it becomes a reality in your life. Start this very day. Find yourself a nice place where you can sit and let your imagination roam. You will see that after dreaming it, you will achieve it.

Make Plans

Some people remain in the planning stages of their dreams. They never take steps to make them come true. You must put your dreams in action. A dream without action is merely an illusion. Many people we know once wanted to do something, but they remained paralyzed. Get up! Get to work. Dream, but act, too.

One day in a Latin American country a young man of about eighteen or nineteen years approached me. As he came toward me, I could see that he was visibly excited about speaking to me. After extending my hand and asking his name, I began listening to his petition. It was one that I had never heard before. He told me that he would like to play the piano like I do, and would I do him the favor of putting my hands on him, taking his hands in mine, and "transfer-ring" (this is the exact word he used) all my knowledge of music to him through a simple prayer. Now, let me state that I am a person who not only believes in miracles, I have seen them with my own eyes, not only in other people's lives, but in my own. Nevertheless, this pe-tition struck me as the limit. What we can acquire with a bit of disci-pline, perseverance, and effort does not require a miracle of God to make happen. Miracles of God should be reserved for those things we mortal beings cannot do. This boy was asking that via a two-minute prayer, I transfer to him years of study, practice, discipline, and effort. With his permission. What a slacker! Yet there are many like him. We want to take a magic pill that will fix everything for us. It doesn't work like that. Knowledge doesn't come to us through osmosis, but through study. Patience is one of the most important ingredients for the development of our dreams. Prepare yourself to achieve what you dream, educate yourself in the areas you're dream-ing of. For example, if you want to sing, do what I did in 1976: I found myself a voice teacher with whom I studied for about four years. Develop a strategy for realizing your dreams and then follow those plans to achieve them. Dreams must be accompanied by action. If there is no action, dreams will never be realized. What's the first ac-tion you need to take? Taking action.

Keep Moving, Don't Stop

Many of us begin the journey toward our objectives with a lot of en-thusiasm, but a lack of persistence makes us give up before we reach our destination. In addition to dreaming and acting, we need to persevere. Perseverance is neither easy nor fun. I assure you that every day when my mom insisted I play piano and review my lessons, it wasn't a task I "wanted" to do, but now, years later, how I thank her for insisting. In fact, when I received my first Latin Grammy, the first person I thanked was my mother. It was because of her patience and effort that I continued in music. If she had not helped me learn perseverance, perhaps I never would have won that Grammy or any other recognition. Thanks, Mom!

With perseverance, even the snail and the worm arrived at Noah's ark. On many occasions, the only thing we can, or know, to do is simply put one foot in front of the other. Maybe things are happening around us that we don't understand, and we ask ourselves if we are in the right place doing what we should be doing. Keep putting one foot in front of the other. Perhaps you are going through a situation of calumny, rejection, or teasing that has taken away your desire to do what you proposed. Keep putting one foot in front of the other. If they have pulled the rug out from under you, making you feel betrayed, creating situations that are difficult to accept, and you have begun to feel like giving up, don't do it. Keep on putting one foot in front of the other. Keep on going to your classes, keeping your promises, being faithful to your word, putting one foot in front of the other, and when you least expect it, you will reach your promised land. I have no doubt about it. Face tomorrow! What awaits you there is extraordinary. Don't look back. There is nothing there for you to conquer. Everything we must conquer lies ahead.

There is a well-known Bible verse that I like a lot which refers to the importance of perseverance. It says: "Let us not become weary in doing good; because in time we will reap a harvest if we do not give up" (Galatians 6:9). The key to reaching the harvest is "to not give up," meaning, those who dismay, desist, or abandon the effort, never reap. Let us not be those who abandon things in the middle. Let's keep putting one foot in front of the other, looking toward the brilliant future that the Lord has prepared for us. There are great triumphs to be achieved. You need to keep walking. History proves that any person who sticks to his dreams for five years will attain them. But many people do not succeed because they give up at four and a half years. Be faithful, persevering, and persistent. The Lord will erase your past and give you a precious future: "He who began the good work in us will perfect it until the day of His arrival" (Philippians 1:6). This is God's promise; for this reason I very much like another phrase of John Mason's that says: "Never dare to trust in an uncertain future over a known God."

For Laughs

In the middle of a huge thunderstorm, on a dark and gloomy night, a guy is standing by the side of a highway, hitchhiking. Time passes, but no one stops. The storm is so strong that he can barely see ten feet in front of him. Suddenly he notices a strange car slowly approach and then come to a stop before him.

Without a moment's hesitation, he gets into the car and

shuts the door behind him. He turns around and to his surprise, realizes the car has no driver.

The vehicle starts up again, smoothly and unhurriedly. The fellow looks out at the highway, and to his horror sees that a curve lies ahead. Frightened, he begins to pray, begging for salvation as he watches his tragic destiny approach. He's still frightened when, just before the curve, he sees a hand reach into the driver's window and move the steering wheel, slowly but firmly.

Paralyzed by terror, he breathlessly clings to his seat with all his might, unmoving and impotent, as he watches the same thing happen at each curve of the dark and horrible road, while the storm grows fiercer. Gathering courage from who knows where, the man jumps out of the car and takes off running to the nearest town. Totally drenched and wandering aimlessly, he heads toward a bar in the distance, walks in, and asks for a strong drink. Still trembling, he begins telling all the customers of the frightful experience he just suffered.

A heavy silence falls on the frightened crowd. Fear fills every corner of the room. In about half an hour, two soaking-wet men walk in, and one says to the other, in an annoyed voice, "Look, John! There's that jerk who climbed into the car when we started pushing it!"

Reflection

1. What dangers, challenges, and unforeseen tests have I been able to confront?

2. In what way can these challenges help me to look toward the future?

3. To which circumstances in the past do I need to remain blind?

4. In what way can I begin to see things as the Lord sees them?

5. How can I leave my comfort zone?

6. How can I begin to put my dreams into action?

Prayer

Dear God, help me to face challenges bravely and break with the lies of fear. I want to remain blind to the past and be able to look toward tomorrow. Help me change my way of thinking and see things the way You do. Give me a new vision and perspective. Help me to keep moving forward and to be persistent. Thank You for Your peace. Thank You because I can trust in You in the midst of affliction, because You have conquered the world.

CHAPTER TEN

The Only Valid Fear

The extraordinary thing about the fear of God
is that when you fear God, you fear nothing else,
while if you do not fear God,
you fear everything else.

—OSWALD CHAMBERS

Although what I am going to say sounds strange, one of the most effective ways to destroy the fear in our lives is by fearing the Lord. It sounds strange because we are talking about destroying fear, and then about having another kind of fear. That's because they are two different types of fear. One fear, the kind we need to overcome, is the fear that comes from fright, terror, and anxiety. The other kind of fear is one of reverence, respect, and honor. Solomon the Wise wrote: "The beginning of wisdom is the fear of God" (Proverbs 1:7). When we respect, honor, and revere the Lord, fear and terror can no longer be a part of our lives, because where God is seated, fear cannot live. It's unfortunate that there are many who have an incorrect notion of what it is to fear the Lord. We need to have a better understanding of how we revere Him by giving Him preeminence in our lives.

Some time ago I read: "Since we have lost the fear of the Lord, the world has been full of fear. We are sick with hundreds of fears, fear of ourselves, fear of others, of the world, of the future. Only he who fears the Lord is free of fear" (author unknown). In the preceding chapter, we learned that God did not give us a spirit of cowardice, but rather one of power, love, and self-control and good judgment. However, it is equally important to recognize that "The beginning of wisdom is the fear of the Lord" (Proverbs 1:7). He who fears the Lord is wise. When we understand what it means to "fear the Lord," we will understand what "the proper fear of God" is. God wants us to walk in wisdom, but to do this we must fear Him. Let's examine what fear of the Lord is, looking first at "what is *not* the fear of God."

What the Fear of God Is NOT

It's interesting to think about why so many people are afraid of the dentist. In most cases, it must be due to a bad experience they had. I know of a woman who said of the dentist from her youth: "I began to feel upset and to cry, and he said to me, 'If you don't be quiet I'm going to slap you.'" It's understandable, then, why today she is ready to travel more than sixty miles to go to a dentist with whom she feels safe. In the same way, it's probable that those who have a fear of God (as opposed to reverential fear of Him) may do so because of a similar reason. It's probable that some of them acquired an unhealthy fear of God when they were children, because of a bad experience with someone who represented God. Still others have used the name of the Lord to frighten or manipulate people. For example, I once heard a mom tell her crying little child that if he was quiet, God wouldn't get angry with him. I asked myself, What kind of person wants his child to grow up with the concept of a god who gets angry when you're crying? This child has certainly asked himself many times, what kind of god is it, then? That mom, because of wanting to manipulate her child to do her bidding, smeared the good image of the Lord in the child's mind. No good! Unfortunately, in today's culture, there are many incorrect ideas about what the fear of God is, thanks to people like that mom who have misrepresented the Lord. I can promise you that the correct fear of the Lord has nothing to do with fright. Nowhere in the Bible does it say that we should "be afraid" of God, but rather "have a fear of God." There is a difference.

When Adam and Eve disobeyed the Lord, they hid in the Garden of Eden because they knew they had committed a grave mistake. They declared: "We were afraid and we hid from You" (Genesis 3:10). When you and I have an appropriate fear of God, it's not an emotion that moves us to hide from Him. Rather, when we know He is looking for us, we run toward Him like a child runs into the arms of a loving father. But in the case of Adam and Eve, they were afraid of the Lord because of the sin they had committed, and that fear does make us run and hide. When we are afraid of Him, the mere sound of His voice causes us to panic.

Some who have represented the Lord have taught us that He is implacable, difficult, irritable, and angry. They bring us mental images of an old man with a wrinkled face, a lined brow, and angry mouth, with a long white beard, a severe gaze, and a club sixty-five feet long in His hand to castigate whomever misbehaves. Over the years, there have been representatives of God who have spoken so much about His judgment and severity that that is the only image that the general public has of Him. It's a true shame, especially when we realize that God is merciful, slow to anger, a giant of compassion, filled with grace and love. The Bible teaches that the Lord is a god of happiness, forgiveness, help, and aid who is always looking for how He can help us get ahead. It says that His compassions are new every day and that He holds us in the palm of His hand. Do you realize how different this picture is from the other? The Lord is a god who smiles. The Lord is a god who sings. He is love.

The fear of the Lord is not about living uneasily, thinking, "I believe the Lord doesn't love me because I misbehaved five years ago." How horrible it would be to live this way! Imagine having to think about all the bad things we've done in our entire lives. God is so good that He says: "If we confess our sins, He is faithful and ready to forgive our sins" (1 John 1:9). People who worry that God is going to punish them for all the wrongs they've done, are going to live in constant anxiety and uncertainty. There is no reason to live this way. The Bible teaches that you and I can go confidently before the throne of grace, without fear, to receive "help in our time of need" (Hebrews 4:16). I am fascinated with the idea of going before the throne of the Lord to ask for help. He promises to give us "timely" help, not whenever He feels like it, but our help will come at the moment we need it most. The Lord is that good to us.

At times, one is like the traffic cop who finds a place to station himself and await speeding motorists. Perhaps he waits in a spot where the highway climbs a small hill and suddenly goes down, creating a blind spot where the driver cannot see the policeman on the other side of the little hill. It's a trap the police set to "surprise" motorists. Many speed addicts have been caught using this kind of strategy. Having a fear of God is not waiting to see if God's law is going to trap me. The Bible says that "the law is for those who are without law." Those who never break the law never need worry about it. Those who are always breaking it are the ones who need to worry. But if you and I walk with rectitude, openly, in the light of day, in obedience and honesty, then we will have nothing to fear. Like the saying goes, "He who owes nothing, fears nothing."

The psalmist David declared the following: "The Lord is my light and my salvation—whom should I fear?" (Psalms 27:1). When he wrote this declaration he did not express it in the meaning of the bravery of a braggart, but simply from a heart full of tranquillity and peace that we who love the Lord and live in the confidence that comes from knowing Him have. The soul who knows the Father is not afraid. Like the psalmist, we can say, "We have no reason to fear anyone. The Lord is our light, our salvation. He will fight our battles. He is on my side. I can be calm and confident." That is the type of confidence that comes from knowing and trusting Him.

What the Fear of God Is

When we contemplate the marvelous works of the Lord, we are left speechless. Looking at the stars, the works of His hands, we are left admiring. That is an aspect of the fear of God—recognizing that my eyes cannot take in the immensity of His enormous and magnificent creation. When I witnessed the birth of my daughter, Elena, I was overcome with an emotion so strong that I don't know how to describe it. My first reaction was to recall the Bible verse that says: "Only the fool says in his heart, there is no God" (Psalms 14:1). It is impossible to see that marvelous creation of the Lord, the miracle of birth, the process itself, the millions of details that must be just right for the birth to turn out well, and even after all that dare to say that there is no God. Only a fool, an idiot, could do so. Only a fool. It's interesting that scientists are still discovering new things about the universe. They are surprised when they discover them. For me, personally, it surprises me that they are surprised. Don't they know how great is our Lord. The psalmist David said: "When I see Your heavens, the works of Your fingers, the moon and the stars that You formed, I say: 'What is a man, that you are mindful of him. And the son of man, that You care for him? You have made him a little less than the angels, and You crowned him with glory and honor. You made him master over the works of Your hands; You put everything under his feet: sheep and oxen, all of it, and likewise the beasts of the fields, the birds in the skies, and the fish in the sea, everything that swims the paths of the ocean. Oh, The Lord, our Father, how great is Your name in all the land!' " (Psalms 8:3–9).

On many occasions when Jesus touched the sick or performed one of His great miracles, His disciples were astonished and the result of the astonishment was the glorification of His name. The people around Him also glorified Him. In the same way, you and I can. When we contemplate how great the Lord has been in our lives, we have no other reaction than to lift up our hands and exclaim in a loud voice: "Thank you, Lord, I glorify You because Your works are great and marvelous in my life! I will praise You because formidable and marvelous are Your works; I am amazed, and my soul knows it well" (Psalms 139:14). This is a dimension of the fear of God—reverent admiration.

Devotional Respect

I meditated on these two little words *devotional respect*, and I recalled the history of Esther. She was a simple young woman in a strange land who suddenly found herself in an interesting situation. She was chosen to be queen during a time of many changes and in the face of a terrible problem. There was a very evil man close to the king who wanted to kill all the Jewish people. Esther was a Jew, and she knew that if she did not intervene, she, along with all of her people, would become history if this man, Haman, got his way. Esther recognized that only she could get out in front of this situation in the name of her people. She chose to break with protocol and go before the king to plead, despite the fact that he had not called for her. She weighed the risk of breaking protocol and decided to go for it. If she died while pleading for her people, she had nothing to lose because she would also die if she did not plead for them. Esther knew that if she found favor in the king's eyes, he would extend his scepter. If he did not, it would mean instant death for her. The story goes that Esther dressed herself in a royal gown, put on perfume, and entered the interior patio of the house of the king. When she went before him, it says she presented herself to him with devotional respect. It was not fear or fright, but devotional respect. While the king looked at her, the miracle that she and her people needed occurred. Esther had found grace in the eyes of the king, who extended his scepter and said: "Esther, what is it you desire?" The end of the story is one of great victory. The evil man Haman ended up dying a tragic death for having conspired against the queen's people. Esther was the heroine who saved all her people from disaster. What gets my attention, however, is the phrase *devotional respect.* She acted with humility and confidence. Just as we do when we have a proper respect of who God is in our lives.

Perhaps we still need to prepare ourselves, like Esther did, before approaching the throne of the Lord. Maybe we need a good bath, to perfume ourselves with the essence of the Word of God, to dress ourselves in the royal garments that Jesus Christ has given us, and *then* approach the interior patio of the house of the King to let Him extend His scepter to us and receive us into His loving arms. We must go toward the King with devotional respect, and when God sees our hearts and we can admire Him, He will extend His scepter to us and good things will happen in our lives. Obviously, devotional respect does not mean being "made equal." Rather it keeps everyone in his rightful place. If the president of a nation were before us, we would show him absolute respect; we wouldn't treat him like a close friend. We would maintain propriety in relation to our respective positions. For this reason we say that when a child speaks to an adult in the familiar form without that trust or that friendship, it is trying to be "equal." That is to say, we don't need to be the Lord's equal, but rather have a relationship of devotional respect toward Him. Maintain our position of trust, without being disrespectful. That is an important part of knowing the fear of God.

In the presence of the Lord there is reverent admiration, a respect for who He is, but there is also trust. If you read the biblical story of Esther, you will discover that there was another queen named Vashti who lost her rule by acting as an equal. The king called for Vashti, but she preferred to keep polishing her nails (an explanatory note: this thing of polishing nails is my imagination in "turbo" mode. I am not sure she was painting her nails, but my imagination helps to understand the disdain she showed the king) (Esther 1:17). Because of this lack of respect toward the king, Vashti lost her position as queen, and in searching for a new queen, the king found Esther (Esther 2:17).

Relational Trust

Saint John the Apostle wrote: "And in this we knew that we have come to know Him, if we keep His commandments" (1 John 2:3). When we move in the commandments of God and walk to the light of His Word, we do so with confidence because we know well it is God who guides us. He promises us that "He will not let your foot slip, nor will He who watches over you slumber" (Psalms 121:3). Thus the psalmist expresses his absolute trust in God. You and I walk in confidence when we do so in the Lord's perfect law. In this way we can achieve what is called "relational trust." Keeping His commandments means keeping His confidence, and when one keeps the confidence there is pleasure in the friendship. Has anyone ever betrayed your confidence? I hope it never happens to you, as it is one of the worst things that can happen. But when we walk with the Lord, we can be sure in our friendship with Him. God will never betray us. Of this we can be completely sure.

One of my personal faults is that I really like driving fast. One time while traveling with my three sons I suddenly asked them, "Boys, do you want to see how fast we can go?" They assured me they did, so when I came to a long straightaway, I began to accelerate. Suddenly, one of my sons said to me: "Dad, it's good Mom is not with us, because she'd surely be scolding you right now." After a hearty laugh, I answered: "Son, if your mom had come with us, she would have the right to scold me because we have relational trust." Our marriage is based on trust. I never worry what my wife will talk about with her friends, because we have a beautiful relational trust between us. Our relational trust is one of the greatest delights of our friendship. It's one of the firm bases of our family. In the same way, our security in God is based on our "relational trust." If things between you and Him are clear, then everything is in order. As the refrain goes: "Clear accounts, long friendships."

The Word of God says: "Let us then approach the throne of grace with confidence, so that we may receive mercy and find grace to help us in our time of need" (Hebrews 4:16). The throne represents majesty, magnificence, and authority, but the throne of our Lord, even though it is majestic, full of light and authority, doesn't cease to be a throne of grace and compassion. We need to have the safety of knowing that if the Lord is with us, "who is against us?" We can walk confidently, admiring the greatness of the Lord, respecting Him devotionally, but trusting in our friendship with Him. These are some of the correct aspects of the fear of God. Stop trembling and begin to enjoy God. Stop being afraid and draw close to the Lord. Let the Lord's arms surround you.

Profound Intimacy

The fear of God is a point of departure for a profound intimacy with God. Many of us, in whichever country we live, know some information about the president of our country. We know something of his political past, his studies, his political activity, but in truth, we don't know him deeply. If I were to encounter him face-to-face, I would know him but he would not recognize me, even though I may know everything about his life and history. I could not approach him as if he were a family member, since that would be disrespectful and irreverent. My knowledge of him does not provide me with relational intimacy. Something similar occurs with fans of rock, film, or sports. They know their "idols," but the celebrities do not know them.

To know God we must be part of a relationship in which He knows us and we know Him. The greater the intimacy established with Him, the greater will be the depth of our relationship. Like in any friendship, the key word is *time*. If we never invest time in a relationship, it will never flourish. If we don't spend time with our families, we will never be friends. If we never spend time with our spouses, the level of intimacy that is needed to maintain a good marriage will never develop. It's the same with the Lord. We will never be able to know Him if we never spend time with Him. We should see it as a vital and fundamental part of the development of our relationship with Him. Time. We need to spend more time with God.

As we have learned up to this point, fear is a fortress that rises in the face of the unknown. At the same time, we understand that

that which we hear will produce faith or fear, and when we plant fear, the harvest will cause torment in our lives. Nevertheless, the more time we spend developing a relationship with the Lord, the less time we spend operating in fear. When we exercise our love for God by doing what He tells us to do, fear abandons our lives. God believes in us and is aware of everything that happens to us. We can go closer "With confidence to the throne of grace to receive mercy and find grace" (Hebrews 4:16).

We began this book talking about how "In love there is no fear, but rather perfect love drives out fear" (1 John 4:18). But upon reaching the end of these pages, I would like to conclude with an absolute affirmation that I hope to sum up in this phrase: "When I can comprehend that all negative emotions come from fear and the positive ones, from love, I will begin to fill myself with the love of the Lord and free myself from fear."

For Laughs

Two restless young brothers aged eight and six went to church faithfully every Sunday with their mother. She was tired of trying to get them to behave during the Sunday service and had the great idea of making an appointment with the pastor of the church. He could talk with the children, in the hopes of helping them understand the importance of behaving well in the meeting place of God. When the morning of the appointment arrived, the mother left them off at the assigned hour and the two children went into the big temple and sat where their mother had told them the pastor would be waiting for them, in the first row. Only a few minutes went by before the pastor appeared, a tall, husky man with a mustache. He grabbed a chair, placed it in front of the children, and sat down. He let a few moments pass before speaking, thus provoking an air of strictness. The two children looked at him with big eyes and could barely breathe, for the fear they felt.

Suddenly the pastor asked them, "Children, where is God?" He did this with the aim of helping the little brothers understand that in church they were in God's house, so they had to respect it and behave well when they were there.

Silence. Neither child could say anything.

Again the pastor asked, "Children, who can tell me where God is?"

Nothing. Their eyes only grew bigger and their hearts beat faster.

For the third time the pastor asked, only this time he moved a little closer to them, and in a grave, hushed voice he again posed his question, "Children, where is God?"

At this, the elder of the two grabbed his younger brother's hand and began to run. They ran out the back door and down the street. They turned left and ran to the corner. Then they turned left again and ran, terrified, for two blocks, sufficiently far away from the place they were fleeing.

"What's wrong?" asked the younger brother.

His older brother answered, "They lost God in that place, and they want to blame it on us."

Reflection

1. How much reverence and respect do I have for the Lord?

2. What place does God have in my life?

3. What is my concept of the fear of God?

4. Have I lost the fear of the Lord?

5. What image do I have of God?

6. Do I have fear or panic about God?

7. What admirable works of God can I contemplate in my life and surroundings?

8. How deep is my intimacy with the Lord?

Final Prayer

Lord, I ask that every erroneous idea about who You are be dissolved at this time, in the name of Jesus. Break apart every lie that has kept so many people imprisoned with false images of a strict and terrible God. Help us to understand who You are and how we can trustingly come nearer to Your throne of grace to receive Your opportune help and be able to walk confidently, free of fear.

ACKNOWLEDGMENTS

Johanna Castillo, a woman of great vision, energy, and brilliant professionalism. Working with you has been a true pleasure. Thanks for pushing me toward excellence.

Gisela Sawin, thank you for the hours of devotion dedicated to this project. Your efforts make you a part of the lives that have been changed thanks to this book.

Amy Greenberg, what an outstanding translation. You are the best! Thanks a million.

Tom Winters, thanks for being a great friend, supporter, and door opener for me. Only heaven will tell how many rewards you will receive for being the quiet, behind-the-scenes planter of blessings that you are.

Wiljosmer Mora, your devotion and dedication to this project made it an outstanding book. Without your contribution, I never would have finished the manuscript by the deadline. Working with you is a pleasure.

Bruce Calderon, thank you for your constant support and dedication. You are a blessing.

Alfonso Ortiz, thank you for always being watchful, vigilant, and for helping me organize my time to complete this project. I am eternally grateful.

Joel and Victoria Osteen, we hadn't started living our best life until we came to Lakewood. Thanks for being such a great example of people who live free of fear.

Elena, Jonathan, Kristofer, and Carlos, thanks for putting up with all the days I was away from home, passionate about shaping this manuscript into the message that God has burned into my bones. You are the best!

Miriam, there is no one like you. I thank the Lord so much for the day I met you. You changed my life and in many ways you keep doing so day after day, even after more than two decades of life together. I love you more each day!

Jesus, Your life was a great example of what a real man is. Your death restored to us the path toward our Father. Your resurrection gives us hope of an eternal life. You are my hero!

BIBLIOGRAPHY

Acosta, Andrea. "Pornography: A Danger Disguised as Pleasure" ("Pornografía: Un peligro disfrazado de placer"), July 17, 2003, El Pregonero, http://www.elpreg.org/noticias/07-17-03/4.shtml.

Bernardo, Rafa, and Juan Carlos Flores. "Phobias of the Famous." ("Fobias de famosos"), Escuela de Periodismo UAM/EL PAIS, http://www.elpais.es/corporativos/elpais/escuela/edp_pa ginas; shtrabajos_alumnos/web2004/webfobias/paginas/fcu famo.htm.

Mantilla, Chalela, and Pablo Alberto, MD. "Social Phobia" ("Fobia social"). Susmedicos.com.http://www.susmedicos.com/art_fo bia_social.htm.

Coloma, Cristina Ruíz. *Dare Not to Be Perfect: When Perfectionism Is a Problem (Atrévase a no ser perfecto: Cuando el perfeccionismo es un problema)*. Barcelona: Editorial Debolsillo, 2003.

Contreras, P Francisco. "Do Not Be Afraid" ("No tenga miedo"), 2006.

Iglesias, Marina. "The Most Unusual Phobias: What They Are and How to Cure Them" ("Cuáles son y cómo se pueden curar las fobias más insólitas"), Imaginarius http://miarroba.com/foros/ver.php?foroid=207474&temaid=2937566.

Kennedy, Daniel. "It's All in Your Mind" ("Todo está en su mente"), 2006.

Lafuente, Henzo. "Dictionary of Phobias" ("Diccionario de fobias"), October 2002, Apocatastasis.com:literature y contenidos selecci-onados http://www.apocatastasis.com/fobias-diccionario.htm.

The Bible, New International Version (La Santa Biblia, Nueva Ver-sion Internacional), International Bible Society (Sociedad Biblica Internacional), 1979.

The Bible (La Santa Biblia, Reina-Valera), Bible Societies in Latin America (Sociedades Biblicas en América Latina).

"Fear and Phobias" ("Los miedos y las fobias"), Enplenitud.com., http://www.enplenitud.com/nota.asp?articuloID51.

"My Cistern Book" ("Mi libro de cisterna"), April 11, 2003. ESKPE.com,http://www.eskpe.com/secc_eskpe/umo_eskpe/ Postres-de_Notas/abrillajuniode2003/ARTICULO-WEB-NO TA_INTERIOR_ESKPE-2101867.html.

Women of the Third Millennium. "Phobia" (Mujeres del tercer milenio, "Fobia"), Luis José Uzcátegui, supervisor. July 25, 2003. Gentiuno, gente del siglo XXI. http://www.gentiuno.com/ articulo.asp?articulo=459.

———. "Panic Disorder" (Mujeres del tercer milenio. "Trastorno de pánico"), July 25, 2003. Gentiuno, gente del siglo XXI. http://www.gentiuno.com/articulo.asp?articulo=458.

"What Is Anxiety/Social Phobia?" ("Qué es la ansiedad/fobia social?"), Socialphobia.net. the portal of Social Phobia (Fobiaso cial.net, el portal de la fobia social), http://www.fobiasocial .net/ansiedad-social.php.

"Mental Health: Be Free at Last" (Salud mental, ser libre al fin"),
September 24, 2005. Help Association (Ayuda Asociación).
http://www.asociacionayuda.org/notas_prensa_noticias.html.

Wallis, Claudia, and Kristina Dell. "What Makes Teens Tick," *Time*,
vol. 163, no. 19, May 10, 2004.

BIBLICAL CITATIONS

Where to Find Advice when:

TEACHINGS ABOUT:

For more information about Marcos Witt please visit:

www.canzion.com

www.marcoswitt.net

Bookings:

Concert: Mauricio Abaroa, mabaroa@aol.com

Speaking: Alfonzo Ortiz, alfonzo@canzion.com

Or write to:

Canzion

914 W. Greens Rd.

Houston, TX 77067

Printed in the United States
By Bookmasters